Pulpit & People

Pulpit & People

Essays in honour of William Still on his 75th birthday

edited by

Nigel M. de S. Cameron
Warden of Rutherford House, Edinburgh

and

Sinclair B. Ferguson
Associate Professor of Systematic Theology,
Westminster Theological Seminary, Philadelphia

RUTHERFORD HOUSE BOOKS
EDINBURGH

Published by Rutherford House,
Claremont Park, Edinburgh EH6 7PJ, Scotland

ISBN 0 946068 18 6 cased
0 946068 19 4 limp
Copyright © 1986 Rutherford House and Contributors
This edition published 1986

Typeset by The Tweeddale Press Group, Berwick upon Tweed.
Printed by Martin's of Berwick.

CONTENTS

CONTRIBUTORS

Montagu G. Barker is Consultant Psychiatrist, Barrow Hospital, Bristol, and Clinical Lecturer in Psychiatry, Bristol University Medical School

Nigel M. de S. Cameron is Warden of Rutherford House, Edinburgh

Sinclair B. Ferguson is Associate Professor of Systematic Theology in Westminster Theological Seminary, Philadelphia, Pennsylvania, USA

Douglas F. Kelly is Associate Professor of Systematic Theology in Reformed Theological Seminary, Jackson, Mississippi, USA

Francis Lyall is Professor of Public Law in the University of Aberdeen, and Clerk to the Deacons' Court in Gilcomston South Church, Aberdeen

J. Douglas Macmillan is Professor of Church History and Church Principles in the Free Church of Scotland College, Edinburgh

I. Howard Marshall holds a Personal Chair of New Testament in Christ's College, University of Aberdeen

Brian Moore is Minister of the West Kirk, Belfast

Rowland Moss is Pro-Vice-Chancellor and Professor of Human Ecology in the University of Salford; and Honorary Curate in the Parish of St Andrew with Emmanuel, Diocese of Chester

George M. Philip is Minister of Sandyford Henderson Memorial Church, Glasgow

James Philip is Minister of Holyrood Abbey Church, Edinburgh

Henry A. G. Tait is Minister of the South Church, Crieff

David F. Wright is Senior Lecturer in Ecclesiastical History in New College, University of Edinburgh

William Still

FOREWORD

The presentation of a *Festschrift* is an unusual way of honouring a minister of the Gospel, but William Still is an unusual man. His ministry has had an incalculable influence on the church of God, in Scotland and far beyond. The wide spread of contributors to this volume bears its own testimony. Teachers of theology from two of the leading north American seminaries are joined by the Pro-Vice-Chancellor of an English university, a consultant psychiatrist, and professors from Aberdeen University itself, to celebrate the 75th birthday of a parish minister. And it is hardly as if this volume were an exhaustive collection of tributes. There could have been many others, and an apology is due to those for whom space precluded an invitation.

The present writer, as Warden of Rutherford House, has special tribute to pay. The trust which established this institution is chaired by William Still. It is a measure of the man that after a lifetime of dogged commitment to the preaching and pastoral ministry he could take a lead in setting up a centre for theological research. His doing so has raised the eyebrows of some who thought the two did not go together, but confounded forever any suggestion that William Still's evangelicalism could be dismissed as anti-intellectual. Indeed, one of the striking features of his ministry has been his ability, as a man who would make no claim to be 'academic', to have a decisive influence on those who plainly are.

The present writer gained his first inkling of the stature of William Still when, as an undergraduate at Cambridge, he was accosted by a famous professor who had once taught at Aberdeen. William Still's name was displayed on a poster giving intimation of a student conference, and the professor asked to be remembered to him. Himself no evangelical, he had heard William Still preach in the University chapel in Aberdeen; and his comment had been, 'I detect the authentic Pauline spirit.' It is, perhaps above all else, the quality of *authenticity* which has drawn so many to WS, and given him such influence with them.

So we pay tribute to one who, under God, has taught us and been to us an example of a man in Christ. On behalf of the many hundreds of his friends the world over, we salute him on his 75th birthday. And we thank God for him.

Rutherford House, Edinburgh
26.i.1986

Nigel M. de S. Cameron

WILLIAM STILL:

a biographical introduction

SINCLAIR B. FERGUSON

William Still was born on the 8th of May 1911, in Aberdeen. Both of his parents, William and Helen Still came from the little fishing village of Gardenstown some forty miles north along the coast from Aberdeen.

His early Christian nurture took place within the context of the Salvation Army Corps, so that by the age of thirteen he was already a decided Christian, eager to find some sphere of service in the kingdom of God. But it was another twenty years before those early aspirations found their chief fulfilment when, in 1945, he was called to his first (and as time has now demonstrated, his only) pastoral charge of the Church of Scotland, Gilcomston South in Aberdeen.

Mr Still once briefly summarised the first half of his life in this way:

> From the age of seven I suffered a series of set-backs in health which seemed by adolescence to confirm my inability to make anything of my life. I tried to work with my father in the fish trade at fourteen, turned to music at seventeen, to Christian service in the Salvation Army at twenty-three, and in six months was in a state of nervous exhaustion. Four years later, somewhat improved in health, I offered for Salvation Army work again, but was rejected on the grounds of health, and immediately decided that I must try to fulfil my, by then, clear call to divine service, elsewhere than in that branch of the Christian Church.

Now, after forty years of ministry in Aberdeen, it is possible for us to look back with him and recognise how characteristically God took one of the weak things of the world to show his own faithfulness and power (1 Cor. 1:18–2:5). Certainly, humanly speaking, had his life taken its intended course, the impact of his ministry would have been very different from what it has been.

Now in his late twenties — having left school at the age of thirteen — he entered the University of Aberdeen, and during the Second World War began his studies for the Church of Scotland ministry, at Christ's College. He then proceeded to Glasgow, as assistant minister to Dr William Fitch, in Springburn Hill Church in the Springburn area of the city. During his year as an assistant (about which there are numerous stories of almost legendary nature!) he was involved in a train accident. He was hospitalised for three months, and thereafter recuperated in Aberdeen. He had already been approached by the "vacancy committee" at Gilcomston South Church, but he had remembered the advice of one of his College Professors never to accept a call to his home town. So he had declined, gratefully but firmly. His recuperation

1

in his home town, however, led to the reversal of that decision. His record of how he changed his mind is intriguing:

> It was while I was hirpling about Aberdeen, first on two crutches, then on one, and on two sticks, then on one, that my maternal aunt Bella, recently widowed, came to the West Church of St Andrew with me one evening for the 7 o'clock service. It was an informal service, and the minister chatted with the people in the aisles afterwards. He saw me and asked what I was going to do. I said 'Erskine Blackburn of Holburn Central Church (who was interim moderator in the Vacancy) has asked if I will accept a call to Gilcomston South. What do you think?' He said 'I wouldn't. My assistant says, "Not even Saint Paul could do anything with that place" . . . .'
> Later that evening, while waiting at the 'bus stop, my aunt asked me, 'What was the minister saying?' I told her. 'And what do you think of that?' she asked. Then, almost casually and with, as I recall it, a far-away tone in my voice and no sense of the dramatic, and certainly no sense of destiny, I replied, 'Maybe less than Paul will do'.

The call was later accepted. The West Church assistant minister had not been engaging in a piece of smart cynicism in his remarks about the condition of the Gilcomston South congregation, whose building stood almost directly across Union Street from the West Church itself. It was war-time. In the event, of the 600 names on the Congregational Roll, only 74 members and 2 adherents were to sign Mr Still's call. Earlier in the 'vacancy', between December 1943 and June 1945, discussions had taken place about the possibility of merging the congregation with another. Only 58 members had been present at the meeting which resolved to continue as a separate congregation, and of that number 18 had voted for union with another congregation, 14 for dissolving the congregation altogether, and only 26 for continuing! These were hardly encouraging statistics for a new minister. But William Still had received a profound sense of conviction that God was calling him to minister in this church. As he often later remarked, that conviction was to carry him through many discouragements, frustrations and disappointments, during the years of ministry which followed.

These past four decades of ministry at Gilcomston South have been notable for many reasons. In fact, this one lengthy ministry has, in several respects, been many ministries, as the congregation has grown in size and Christian maturity, and as its membership has changed over the years. Even the emphases in the pulpit and in the style of church life have developed. New avenues of service have opened up, and new burdens for prayer and concern. As Mr Still once wrote in a congregational letter:

> No man and congregation can go on year after year doing the same things and keep alive unless there is not only change, but sequence, rhythm, and (we hope) progress towards solid spiritual achievement, that not only meets the need of our day, but points forward, prophetically, to the spiritual needs of tomorrow and to a new generation.

The first months of ministry, in the aftermath of the War, were marked by a flood of evangelistic activity. This partly coincided with a remarkable visit to Aberdeen by the then young and relatively unknown American evangelist, Billy Graham. Two meetings were held in the church in 1946, during one of which the following interchange took place:

> I took the opening prayer . . . . When I returned to my seat in the choir pew, I found myself seated next to Billy. In his expansive human way he turned and put his arm round me and whispered, 'Will you come to America?' 'Just like that?' I asked. 'Yes' he said . . . .

But William Still did not go to America (either then, or later!). He did, however, throw all his energies into a series of Saturday night gatherings for young people, held in the church. These 'rallies' had everything: choirs, organ, piano, solos, testimonies, sermons! Hundreds crowded into the sanctuary and many dated their Christian beginnings from those meetings. Large numbers of military cadets were among them. People were 'falling into the Lord's lap like plums', Mr Still later wrote. Suddenly Gilcomston South seemed to have come to life; financially it began to prosper, and within a couple of years givings had quadrupled. From many points of view the new ministry was all that could have been hoped for. It seemed that, after all, a 'lesser than Paul' had managed to do something with Gilcomston South!

Parallel to this excitement, however, came a transformation in William Still's own thinking. As if by accident he had begun to do something during the Sunday services which — although he did not then know it — had first been done by the great preachers of the early church and of the Reformation. He had begun to preach in a consecutive and systematic way through the Bible. Even although he did not then recognise the precedent for what he was doing, he knew that there was a new depth and penetration in his preaching, and a character-forming power in God's word, which made these other services seem somewhat superficial by comparison. He became convinced that the work to which God was now calling him was the building of strong Christian character through the patient teaching and preaching of the whole word of God.

He took a radical decision. Abandoning the Saturday night 'rallies' he began a meeting for prayer instead. The effect was instantaneous and numerically dramatic. Between one Sunday evening and the next, the congregation at the evening service *dropped* by between two and three hundred. So upset were some people in the city that they accused him of driving the young people out of the church and into the cinemas on a Saturday night! His answer — which he wisely refrained from giving — was that there was nothing hindering them coming to pray. What better way for a Christian to spend the evening?

But Mr Still had stumbled on something which was to leave an indelible impression on him: even given personal differences over the wisdom or otherwise of this change, the challenge to become a man or woman of prayer, to share in the very nerve centre of the church's life, is one from which many turn away in order to stand on more convenient ground. From that time until today, his ministry has been to smaller rather than larger congregations. From the beginning, or virtually the beginning of his ministry, he has set his heart on quality, even if it should be at the expense of quantity. The fact that the Gilcomston prayer meeting has continued to convene for two hours of prayer each Saturday night for forty years is a testimony to his commitment to that early principle.

This determination has been coupled with a commitment to another principle: the chief task of the pastor is to guard and tend his own flock. From the 1940's until now, Mr Still has consecrated his entire life to the people of his flock. Indeed as early as 1948 he wrote to them:

> I have cut out every external activity and interest, and every moment of my time is solely devoted to the work of Gilcomston and the needs of its wider congregation (apart from such engagements beyond the bounds of the city as are approved). There is no part of me, or of my life, that I will withhold from the work that God has called me to, and I am determined that no mere form or convention will hinder me from giving the message in the church in a way that will be understood even by the most unlettered person.

This commitment has at times reached unusual lengths. When, in 1974, he actually *declined* the increasingly rare honour of the award of the degree of Doctor of Divinity from the University of Aberdeen, and was asked by a friend for the reason, he simply replied that he did not want his people to be having to call him 'Doctor' after so many years as 'plain Mr'. Perhaps there were other reasons, but he was resolved that nothing should ever divert him from his primary and all-demanding task of serving Jesus Christ by serving his people.

One of the chief features of William Still's life (and a feature which binds together the contributors to this *Festschrift*) has been his special care for young men and women during their student years — either at Aberdeen University, or through one or other of the Christian Union groups in the British Universities and Colleges. To hundreds of us he has been friend, pastor, example and encourager. To dozens of ministers, both in and beyond the Church of Scotland, he has been the *pastor pastorum*, the ministers' minister. Like Christ, the Chief-Shepherd, of whom he once wrote, 'He always had time for the individual . . . and always made them feel that they were worthy of his closest attention', William Still has cared for others. Those of us who have been the happy recipients of that care present to him in the following pages a small token of our affection and care for him, and our gratitude to God for his ministry to us and to all the people of God.

EXPOSITORY PREACHING:

an historical survey

JAMES PHILIP

The impact and influence of the ministry of William Still on the last four decades throughout the Church in Scotland and far beyond has been, on any estimate, immense and far-reaching, in nothing more than in the pattern it has set for systematic, continuous exposition of the Scriptures, and on none, probably, more than on the present writer who gladly acknowledges his sense of indebtedness to his 'father-in-God' and counts it a privilege to participate in this *Festschrift,* on the occasion of his seventy-fifth birthday.

The substance of the brief paper which now follows owes its origin to the reading, some years ago, of a biography of J. P. Struthers of Greenock, a remarkable Scottish 'worthy', and notable preacher and evangelist (1851-1915). Struthers maintained a friendship and correspondence over the years with James Denney, of Trinity College, Glasgow. It was the reading of some of the letters that passed between them, particularly Struthers' request to Denney to send him some of his sermons, and 'a text to preach on next Sunday' that led to the realisation that so much of the preaching of those days was 'textual preaching', that this was in fact the pattern followed by many, if not most, of the prominent evangelical figures of the 19th century, such as R. Murray McCheyne, the Bonars, and Spurgeon. A large part of the preaching of the 18th century also and much of that of the 17th seems to have been of this sort, in contrast to that of the early Church and also of Calvin (and some of the other Reformers) who pursued a policy of systematic exposition of the Scriptures, preaching through the entire Bible in the space of ten years.

Even a cursory examination of this phenomenon of changing patterns in preaching makes it clear that there are some basic presuppositions underlying it in terms of the real nature of preaching. It is the purpose of this essay to examine, however sketchily, the historical development of the Church's preaching from its earliest origins in the Scriptures, through the early centuries of Church history, in the Middle Ages, at the Reformation and in post-Reformation times, down to the present day.

Preaching in Scripture and in the Early Church

Preaching has an ancient lineage. From earliest times in the Old Testament, we have the conception of a priestly function being fulfilled by the father in the family, ministering God's word to them, bestowing the divine blessing upon the firstborn, expounding the mercy of the covenant to his children, and assuming the responsibilities of the priesthood, before a formal priesthood and cultus were established in Israel. Enoch, the seventh from Adam, is said to have prophesied (Jude 14); Noah is termed 'a preacher of righteousness' (2 Pet. 2:5); in patriarchal times the blessings of Isaac and Jacob (Gen. 27:27-29; Gen. 49:3-27) constitute solemn religious addresses. In the time of Moses, when elders were appointed to help him, it is said that 'When the Spirit rested upon them, they prophesied, and did not cease' (Num 11:25). The book of Deuteronomy is a series of addresses by Moses, repeating and expounding much of the legislation given earlier to the people of God.

Later still, we find Joshua uttering his farewell discourses to the assembled congregation in what could fairly be called sermonic form, based on the facts of God's dealings with them in the past, and the reality of the covenant into which he had entered with them. At the end of the period of the Judges, God raised up Samuel, and made him his mouthpiece to Israel, and the word of the Lord came to the people through him in a prophetic ministry that changed the face of the land. Still later in Israel's history, we find king Jehoshaphat, in the context of widespread, national reforms, instituting a programme of teaching throughout Judah, in which the book of the law was expounded to the people (2 Chron. 17:7 ff). And in the whole, distinctive prophetic activity from then until the exile, we have conspicuous and impressive examples of prophetic teaching, as men sent from God ministered his living word to their day and generation.

One very clear and obvious evidence of preaching as exposition of Scripture is found in post-exilic times, in the synagogue service which came into its own during the exile as a substitute for the temple and its worship. The famous passage in Nehemiah 8 records how Ezra the scribe 'stood upon a pulpit of wood which they had made for the purpose, and read in the book of the law of God distinctively, and gave the sense, and caused [the people] to understand the reading'.

This ancient lineage in Scripture for preaching lends credence to Calvin's view that the preaching of the Word belongs, with the institutions of marriage and government, to the natural order, or order of creation. For from the beginning God has revealed himself as a speaking God, a God who wills to have communion with his creatures, making himself known to them in grace and love. There is little doubt that from the earliest dawn of revealed history the divine means of communication with man has been preaching in some form or another, that indeed the communication of the divine grace has been in this way. R. S. Wallace maintains that Calvin 'sees in the prominent place given to the preaching and hearing of the word of God within the Church, a restoration of the true order of nature, for we were given the power to communicate with one another "not simply to buy boots and shoes and bonnets, and bread and wine, but to use our mouths and ears to lead each other to the faith that rises heavenwards to the contemplation of God Himself".'[1]

It is clear that our Lord himself stood in this tradition, when he ministered in the synagogue at Nazareth, and expounded the well-known messianic passage in Isaiah 61 to the people, claiming that it was fulfilled in their ears that day. This is an important indication of our Lord's continuity with the old order, albeit the authority with which he spoke was something new and radical, and sufficient to break through the rigid framework of the past, like new wine bursting old bottles. The nature of that authority was that in his teaching a confrontation took place, in which he, the Lord of the Scripture, met with his hearers and challenged them as the rightful Lord of their lives. It was this that was destined to become the pattern for all New Testament preaching that was to follow.

Above all, however — and this is of supreme importance from the point of view of the establishment of an apostolic pattern of preaching — our Lord's ministry was steeped in Scripture. It could be said that in the truest and deepest sense he lived and taught by the Word. In so doing he was simply being true to himself, for of these Scriptures he said 'They are they which testify of me'. After the resurrection he expounded to the disciples 'in all the Scriptures the things concerning himself', 'opening their understanding that they might understand the Scriptures'.

Whether or not the disciples followed this pattern on the one or two occasions during his earthly ministry when they were sent out two by two by him to preach — there is no reason to suppose they did not — it is certain that after Pentecost they did so, as the recorded 'sermons' in Acts make clear. These consist of a brief account of the life, ministry, death and resurrection of Jesus, according to the Scriptures, and in fulfilment of them, on the basis of which the proclamation of the good news of the gospel of forgiveness through his name was made.

Two things may be said about this. On the one hand, this was the 'pattern' on which the gospels themselves were written; on the other, it follows with great accuracy the development of our Lord's own ministry in the days of his flesh. For it can truly be said that his ministry consisted of two parts, bisected by the great watershed of the Caesarea Philippi confession: before that point, his concern was, by miracle, wonder and sign, by word and action, to show that he was the Messiah promised by Scripture. After that point he was intent on teaching, again from Scripture, that 'the Son of man must suffer and be crucified'. The faithfulness of the apostolic proclamation to this twofold emphasis is impressive, as may be seen from the description of Paul's habitual practice given in Acts 17:2,3, 'opening and alleging that the Christ must indeed have suffered, and risen again from the dead, and that this Jesus, whom I preach, is the Christ'.

Inherent in this pattern is a basic simplicity that is integral to the true

1. R. S. Wallace, *Calvin's Doctrine of the Christian Life*, Grand Rapids, 1961, p. 143 f.

biblical doctrine of preaching, and it is amply evidenced in such passages as Acts 8:4 ff, a passage which may well be taken as a fair indication of the apostolic practice which obtained in the early post-pentecostal era. It can hardly be gainsaid that for the New Testament church, preaching was the most important of all its activities, that it was central to its life, and that it was the source of its spiritual vitality and well-being. This has its own message for those ages of church history, including our own time, in which the church has lost the vision of the power and effectiveness of preaching, and in losing it has lost sight and use of the weapon of spiritual warfare which is mighty through God to the pulling down of strongholds.

The opening up of the Scriptures concerning Christ — such was the legacy left by the early church to posterity; and this must necessarily be the yardstick and criterion by which authentic Christian preaching in any age must be assessed.

From the New Testament to Chrysostom and Augustine

The subsequent history of the Christian church, however, down the years shows only too clearly that the high dignity of this pattern was often but indifferently maintained, and sometimes and for long periods obscured and lost altogether. To be sure, the essential simplicity of New Testament preaching and proclamation was preserved and continued in the immediate post-apostolic age, although there is scant documentary evidence to enable the formulation of a reasonable history of its development. But it is true to say that it took the form of a homily (from the Latin *homilia,* meaning 'a conversation', the word appearing for the first time in a letter from Ignatius to Polycarp to describe the word spoken to the congregation), which was essentially a simple, unpretentious address, spoken extempore, although not without preparation, with little in the way for formal structure. The similarity of this pattern to our Lord's preaching in the synagogue at Nazareth (Luke 4:16 ff) is evident, and it is hardly surprising that it became well established and flourished in the early patristic age, as may be seen in what is possibly the earliest example of the homily, the second epistle of Clement (c. 135-140), and in Justin Martyr's First Apology.

It was as time went on that there was a gradual progression towards a more orderly structure and a more expository character. Historians of the period agree that the movement towards this received its most significant impetus through men like Clement of Alexandria (c. 160-220) and his distinguished pupil Origen (183-254), particularly the latter, who was unquestionably a figure of immense and definitive significance in the early church. It was through him, as one historian maintains, that 'exegesis and preaching were so firmly united that throughout the history of the ancient church and long afterwards they remained intertwined'. His influence was indeed seminal, in that it set a pattern which was followed and developed increasingly from his time onwards to that of the great and significant figures of Chrysostom (344-407) and Augustine (354-430), with whom the full flowering of the ancient homiletical preaching took place, representing respectively the Greek and Latin branches of the church.

Notwithstanding this immense impact, however, it has to be said that other influences were also at work, which bedevilled and finally obscured the original homiletic pattern of the New Testament. One was, sadly enough, a direct result of what may be called the allegorical method of interpretation, popularised by Origen himself — a more fateful influence, and very different from the definitive direction he gave to the true expository method, finding not only double, but treble and even quadruple meanings in Scripture. In this way the possibility of real exegesis was destroyed: the basic rule of interpretation that everything must mean something else than the merely explicit or obvious led to uninhibited and all too often absurd spiritualisations, and this was one of the major factors in making the Bible a sealed book, finally leading the church to believe that Bible-reading was much too perilous a business for ordinary lay people.

Another influence was that exercised by classical rhetoric, which was in the early Christian centuries a term synonymous with higher education, and by which the preachers of the gospel in the post-apostolic age seemed to become increasingly influenced, possibly in the interests of making the appeal of the gospel in the chief seats of learning and governmental power more persuasive. But the adoption of the oratorical devices long familiar to the Greeks and Romans is what the apostle Paul so expressly disavows in his famous warning in 1 Cor. 2:4 about 'the enticing words of man's wisdom', and represents, not an advance from a more primitive and untutored method to a sophisticated and educated one worthier of the gospel and more likely to enhance its power and appeal, but on the contrary a declension from a biblical pattern which led inevitably to the impoverishment of the church's life.

A third contributory factor in this gradual declension was the growth in liturgy and forms of worship which led to the spoken word having, and being given, far less relative value and, still later, to confining it within the liturgical context of the Mass, a process which constricted and impoverished it and finally relegated it to a place so minor as to be practically irrelevant in the life of the church.

All in all, therefore, the age of Chrysostom and Augustine represented a peak in the ascendancy of preaching; and after this time, and due to the factors already mentioned that were present even before this ascendancy, decline set in. Following their time, and onwards through the Middle Ages, up to the time of the Reformation, the whole concept of preaching both in form and content underwent fundamental changes. It is not that during these centuries there was no preaching, for preaching was revived from time to time through the labours of Dominican and Franciscan friars, among others, but on the whole it degenerated to a mechanical level, lacking in true inspiration. And a combination of the above considerations with the fact that Christianity became the official religion of the Roman empire in the time of Constantine meant that conditions favourable to the progress of preaching increased, Christianity became 'respectable' and with the development of worship in elaborate and attractive forms culturally, preaching gradually became more formal and stately. 'The development of preaching,' as one historian observes, 'towards an oratorical form became an integral part of the general ecclesiastical movement.'

With this, the influence of classical oratory began inevitably to make itself felt. As one historian says, 'In the traditional and accepted education system rhetorical studies occupied the chief place. If educated at all, a man was educated in rhetoric . . . . so when the schools were opened to Christians, without persecution or social disfavour, there was opportunity for them to receive the customary oratorical training from the best teachers . . . . also, their hearers were so educated. There was a demand for oratory and rhetoric, and the Church tended to oblige.' Already, by the time of Chrysostom the cult of popular preachers and sermon tasting had become established; and soon when the influence of the scholastic theology of the universities, which from the beginning were clerical institutions, took over, the decline of the ancient, traditional preaching was inevitable: the speculative tendencies of Aristotelian logic in its application to the interpretation of Scripture imposed an intolerable burden upon preaching which virtually destroyed it as an effective means for communicating the gospel.

The mediaeval Schoolmen's patterns of preaching, moreover, became incredibly complex, with all manner of ramifications, divisions and sub-divisions, showing a punctiliousness that to the modern mind is not only artificial but ludicrous. What T. H. L. Parker calls the 'amazingly complicated and subtle form' which they gave to the sermon was rigid and artificial, and it is scarcely surprising that such a pattern became increasingly superficial and powerless. Both content and seriousness of purpose were lost, and preaching sank into an inevitable decay, which had the touch of death upon it.

The Reformation

The time of the Reformation saw a marked, indeed fundamental change. The antecedents of the movement that was destined to revolutionise the whole of Europe go as far back as Wyclif and his Lollard bands, who initiated what Dargan calls 'that wave of mighty reformatory preaching' in the later part of the fourteenth century. It was Wyclif who first departed decisively from the mediaeval pattern, both in form and content, returning to the homily and making preaching once again, as in the early patristic age, the exposition of the Scriptures. It was this noble heritage that was passed on, through John Hus, to Luther and other Reformers, and that became under God the foundation of the Reformation. It was an idea whose hour had come; for Wyclif's Lollards travelled the length and breadth of England, spreading the message of the gospel and making known the Word of God to the common people through the use of Wyclif's translation of the Scriptures into the English language. It was a movement that gathered momentum and became ultimately irresistible, and the Reformation became a glorious fact, setting the whole of Europe aflame with its liberating message of grace.

The transformation in preaching was astonishing. It would not be too much to say that it came into its own in a way that had not been known since the fifth century. It is certainly no accident that Chrysostom and Augustine were the fathers to whom the Reformers looked back with great approval, for they unquestionably stand in that early tradition.

But while it may be true that it was Luther who first 'rediscovered both the form and the substance of this preaching' (Parker), it was supremely in the Reformed, as distinct from the Lutheran, tradition that the continuous exposition of Scripture, brought again into its own by Origen and confirmed by Chrysostom and Augustine, found its fullest expression and reached its greatest heights. The output of the Reformers was prodigious, and makes it clear just what a central place preaching now had in the life of the church. Calvin and Zwingli in particular, with Bullinger following them, preached continuously through books of the Bible, often in the greatest detail, as may be seen from the large number of sermons on particular books.

The implications of this revolution can hardly be over-estimated. With the preaching of the Word being recognized as the primary task of the ministry, preaching resumed its proper place in worship; the Mass was 'dethroned from its usurped reign in the Church', and 'the pulpit, instead of the altar became the central point' in the Reformed churches. 'Preaching was bound to the Scriptures, both in form and in substance. The purpose of preaching, the Reformers said, was to lay bare and interpret the Word of God in Scripture. Hence they set up the Scripture as the criterion by which all their preaching must be judged.'[2] Preaching became more prominent in worship than it had been since the fourth century.

We must now turn our attention to two matters in particular which have a direct bearing on our theme, both integrally related, and emerging from what has been said: (i) the basic presuppositions underlying the essential need felt by the Reformers to make a clean break with the mediaeval scholastic form of preaching and return to the earlier, patristic model, the expositional homily; and (ii) the Reformed doctrine of preaching itself.

(i) Over against the situation that obtained in the mediaeval church, in which the Bible had become a sealed book, because of the alleged

2. T. H. L. Parker, *The Oracles of God*, London, 1947, p. 21.

difficulty, not to say impossibility, for ordinary, untrained people, of studying the Scriptures without the danger of error, the Reformers resolutely believed and taught the essential *perspicuity* or intelligibility of Scripture to the ordinary spiritual mind. John Knox's words to Mary, Queen of Scots make this point well:

> The Word of God is plain in itself; and if there appear any obscurity in one place, the Holy Ghost, Who is never contrary to Himself, explains the same more clearly in other places: so that there can remain no doubt, but to such as remain obstinately ignorant.

Elsewhere, in *A Most Wholesome Counsel,* written in July 1556 to his brethren in Scotland 'touching the daily exercise of God's most holy and sacred Word', Knox speaks of the need to study widely, reading whole books at a time — 'ever ending such books as ye begin (as the time will suffer)' — and to 'join some books of the Old, and some of the New Testament together; as Genesis and one of the Evangelists, Exodus with another, and so forth'.

Here, as J. S. McEwen points out, we have, admirably stated, the essentials of the Reformed doctrine of the *perspicuitas* of Scripture. He adds:

> The Bible is not a rag-bag of assorted proof-texts, as the mediaeval church had made it: it is a unity of revelation, and is to be read in the light of the revelation which it, itself, communicates. Take it where you will, it tells — chapter after chapter — the one story of God's unfolding plan of redemption. Isolated sentences torn from their context, may well be unintelligible or even misleading; but their meaning will become plain when they are read as parts of that great story. Therefore read widely to learn the story, before reading narrowly to elucidate the meaning of single texts.

It is true that in the above-mentioned *Wholesome Counsel* Knox is referring to the reading of the Scriptures; but this does not mean, and Knox does not suggest, that the man in the pew can dispense with the man in the pulpit.

> Knox is well aware that the ordinary believer may have neither the time nor the ability to reach that conspectus of all Scripture which is essential to a balanced interpretation of the Faith in its wholeness, for the well-being of the Church and of the individual believers who require to hear the Word in its wholeness for their edification to the faith, the labours of trained exegetes, theologians and skilled preachers are essential.
> But the perspicuitas of Scripture did mean this: that the wayfaring men, though fools, would meet their God in the Bible, hear His voice, take His promises and comforts and rebukes personally and directly to themselves, and understand enough of what was being said to them to receive, by faith, salvation.

The profound significance of all this can scarcely be exaggerated, in relation to the Reformers' adoption of, or rather reversion to, the continuous exposition of Scripture practised in the early centuries of the Christian era. On the one hand — and this was particularly true at the time of the Reformation — there was a clamant need for a knowledge of the Scriptures to be imparted to the common people.

They had been denied it for so long, and now men were hungry for the Word of life. How else could that knowledge be imparted, except by the most comprehensive exposition of all its parts? On the other hand — and this is even more basic and fundamental — the Reformers maintained that Christ and the Scriptures were inseparable, in the sense that it is only in and through the Scriptures that Christ can be known. Therefore to communicate a whole Christ and mediate a whole salvation, a whole Bible is necessary, for Christ is in all the Scriptures. 'Search the Scriptures', said our Lord, 'for in them ye think ye have eternal life; and they are they which testify of me' (John 5:39).

It can hardly be controverted that in respect to both these considerations, the wheel has come round full circle; for today, there is a widespread ignorance of the Scriptures throughout the land, and — thankfully — a growing awareness of the need for a presentation of the message of the whole biblical revelation with a view to the production of a balanced and mature Christian character in the lives of God's people.

(ii) The indissoluble bond between Christ and the Scriptures has significance for the Reformers' doctrine of preaching also, for indeed the one is the corollary of the other. T. H. L. Parker discusses this at some length in a fine chapter of his book on Calvin, and sums up the distinctive characteristics of the great Reformer's position:

Preaching is the Word of God, first, in the sense that it is an exposition and interpretation of the Bible, which is as much the Word of God as if men 'heard the very words pronounced by God himself';

Secondly, preaching is the Word of God because the preacher has been sent and commissioned by God as his ambassador, the one who has authority to speak in His name;

Thirdly, preaching is the Word of God in the sense that it is Revelation. It is the Word of God when God speaks through the human words, revealing Himself through them and using them as the vehicle of His grace.

To use Calvin's own words, 'He deigns to consecrate the mouths and tongues of men to His service, making His own voice to be heard in them'; and 'Whenever God is pleased to bless their labour, He makes their doctrine efficacious by the power of His Spirit; and the voice which is in itself mortal, is made an instrument to communicate eternal life'. It is not so much that Calvin identifies the spoken, human word with the living Word of God — the distinction between the two is always there — but rather that he recognises that God is pleased to speak in the word that is preached, as indeed is made clear in the important message in Acts 10:44: 'While Peter yet spake these words, the Holy Ghost fell on all them that heard the word'. In other words, the Holy Spirit is given in the preaching of the Word (i.e. when true preaching takes place, for it can never be taken for granted, as a matter of course, that this anointing takes place every time a man chooses to speak forth the truth of the gospel — orthodoxy of doctrine of itself does not guarantee the unction of the Spirit), making the word spoken a living word from on high that creates faith, mediating forgiveness and newness of life.

There are two necessary corollaries or implications of this doctrine of preaching. One is that it is the *preaching*, rather than the preacher, that is of decisive importance, the message rather than the man. Far from 'new presbyter' being 'old priest writ large', a familiar enough accusation, he is in fact the 'servant of the Word', and it is the Word, not the man, that makes the impact and accomplishes the work of grace in men's lives. This is of greater significance than is often realised. If the gospel were, of course, simply a story to relate, then the important consideration would be the preacher — his style, his presentation, his oratory. But if it is, as the Apostles and Reformers held, the power of God unto salvation, and not simply something attended by the power of God, then the emphasis necessarily passes from the preacher to the thing preached, and from the 'excellency of speech' and the 'enticing words of man's wisdom' to the message that comes 'in demonstration of the Spirit and of power'.

The other corollary of the biblical doctrine of preaching is that since it is God that speaks to men in the proclamation of the Word, no man, however spiritually mature or sanctified, is ever in a position of no longer needing that ministry or submitting himself in obedience to it. Parker sums up the Reformer's attitude thus:

> None may think that he has advanced beyond the necessity of hearing preaching because he is able to interpret the Bible for himself. No doubt if preaching were merely a man giving spiritual advice to his religious inferiors, then the spiritually advanced would no longer need this help; but since in preaching God Himself speaks to men, no one may say that he knows sufficient or is sanctified beyond need of help from God.[3]

A greater appreciation of this important truth would surely serve to deliver the people of God from the cardinal error of confusing the proclamation of the Word of God with an exercise in public speaking, to be assessed, judged, criticised and even patronised, instead of accepted humbly and joyfully in a spirit of obedience and submission as a word from on high. The Apostle Paul says it all in his memorable words to the Thessalonians:

> For this cause thank we God without ceasing, because, when ye received the word of God which ye heard of us, ye received it not as the word of men, but as it is in truth, the word of God, which effectually worketh also in you that believe.

The Post-Reformation Scene

It is all the more surprising, therefore, in view of what has been said, that yet again the early homiletical exposition of Scripture should have been departed from in the later 17th century, and onwards, almost to our own time. Even a cursory examination of the preaching in the

3. T. H. L. Parker, *The Oracles of God*, London, 1947, p. 61.

various traditions, Reformed, Lutheran, Puritan, Anglican and Presbyterian obliges one to conclude that the characteristic method of Calvin and his associates was eventually superseded by other and very different patterns of preaching. This is not to say that post-Reformation preaching became barren or moribund; indeed, it is certainly true to say that 'the British pulpit of the 17th century was a living factor of the age' (Dargan), and that it dominated public life in many of its aspects. But it is also true to say that it was subject to influences that served to detach it from the earlier simplicity of the Reformers', and indeed of the Apostles' insights. One historian comments,

> In the course of the [17th] century, it is possible to say, the sermon passed from a period in which its form and content were governed by certain rhetorical and homiletical ideals to a period when it became almost a province of literature, in so far as conformity to the prevailing literary standards was required also from the preacher.[4]

Another historian confirms this view in a fine and perceptive analysis of the influence of the French classical sermon:

> Unquestionably it contributed mightily towards a heightening of the prestige of spiritual oratory since it was not until the nineteenth century that sermons ceased to be classed as literature. But from other perspectives we may raise the question whether or not this influence was sound, whether or not it rather led preaching astray.[5]

In a brief summary of the preaching of Jacques Saurin (1677-1730), the Huguenot preacher, by common consent one of the greatest of the Reformed preachers of the time, he has this to say:

> In Saurin, however, the Calvinistic proclamation experienced a thorough transformation both in content and form. For him, the orthodox Calvinistic formulations had lost their meaning. He was less the disciple of Calvin than the creator of the modern Reformed sermon . . . . He wished to be faithful to Scripture, but he replaced the old expository homily by a sharply logical and cogently argued address in which the short text, often a single verse of Scripture, was subservient to the subject.[6]

This transition is seen clearly in much of Puritan preaching, and it has to be conceded that textual preaching came into its own in the great Puritan tradition. At the same time, however, this tended to lead to very complex and often very involved — and sometimes seemingly endless — patterns of divisions and sub-divisions, which bear a striking resemblance to the mediaeval, scholastic 'arts of preaching' *(artes praedicandi)* more than to Calvin's and the early Reformers' simple homiletic style.

Understandable reactions against the stiff, formal pedantry of this later Puritan method did not, however, lead to a return to Calvin's pattern; for the impact of the Enlightenment began to be felt, and even when the notable influence of men like John Tillotson represented an

4. W. F. Mitchell, *English Pulpit Oratory*, London, 1932, p. 46.
5. Y. T. Brilioth, *A Brief History of Preaching*, Philadelphia, 1965, pp. 147, 148.
6. Y. T. Brilioth, *op. cit.*, p. 158.

15

emancipation from the somewhat stifling and needlessly complex preaching patterns in the interests of simplicity and homiletic plainness, the end-result of that emancipation was ominous. Charles Smyth, in *The Art of Preaching* maintains that the Anglican piety of the 18th century under his influence became 'a piety that had digested Revelation into Reason, and consequently took little interest in Christian Doctrine except as a support for Christian Ethics'. Smyth's conclusion is,

> As recast by Tillotson, the sermon lost its heroic note, and became a moral essay, the vehicle of a sober, utilitarian, prudential ethic, rather than a proclamation of the Gospel of the Kingdom of God. In the hands of his contemporaries it had seemed indeed to belong to literature altogether, rather than to homiletics.

Much more could be said, and indeed would need to be said, about the influences that shaped 18th century preaching, and left their mark on that of the 19th century, a task well beyond the scope of this essay. But it is fair to say that even in the best evangelical preaching of these two centuries — as for example in Charles Simeon in the 18th (1759-1836) and Charles Haddon Spurgeon (1834-1892) — it was the classical, Puritan tradition, which grew out of the *artes praedicandi* of the Middle Ages that was followed, rather than the simple homily of the Reformers, and those who followed Calvin's practice of systematic, consecutive exposition of the Scriptures in these centuries — and indeed in the 20th century, up to the present day — have been conspicuous as exceptions rather than the norm.

It is to be hoped that those in our own day who have the vision of the dynamic potential that this method represents will exercise an increasing influence on the preaching ministry of the late 20th century. It can hardly be controverted that so far as the circumstances which led the Reformers to this pattern are concerned, the wheel has come round full circle: the need is great today — as then — in face of the widespread ignorance of the Scriptures throughout the land, and nothing less than a systematic and comprehensive unfolding of the message of the Scriptures will serve to combat that ignorance, and provide the dynamic for reformation and renewal. Without this, the process of decay in the life of the church is likely to continue, and its future history likely to be short.

THE RECOVERY OF CHRISTIAN REALISM

in the Scottish Expository Ministry Movement

DOUGLAS F. KELLY

'And this is life eternal, that they might know thee, the only true God, and Jesus Christ, whom thou hast sent' (John 17:3).
'So then death worketh in us, but life in you' (1 Cor. 4:12).

Christian theology holds that a finite human being can genuinely know the infinite God directly: this is the essence of what is meant by 'realism'.[1] At first glance it might be objected: why does an article need to be written on this, since all orthodox Christian churches accept it? Do not the first four Ecumenical Councils of the undivided Catholic Church as well as the major Reformed Confessions all profess the realist position, which is, after all, the presupposition of the Holy Scriptures? One must answer, 'Yes, but . . .'.

Our particular church may well claim a certain allegiance to a sound confession, not to mention the Holy Scriptures, but would an honest appraisal show us living in accordance with the truth we corporately confess? If, as Scripture so clearly teaches, we are indeed engaged in an unseen spiritual battle directed from the heavenlies (Ephesians 6), it should not surprise us that given the fallen nature of man outside of Christ, indwelling sin in the believer, plus the pull of a godless world system and the presence of a Satanic kingdom ('the world, the flesh, and the devil' according to 1 John), the church is constantly tempted to think and live on some basis other than 'the truth as it is in Jesus'. Granted that true knowledge of God means nothing less than eternal life (John 17:3), should it surprise us that the enemy of men's souls will mass all his power to keep the church from knowing in heart and action the Triune God whom she professes with her lips?

For much of its history (except perhaps during times of major revival), the church has been tempted to veer away from a real knowledge of God in Christ by going astray in either one of two different directions. We may, somewhat simplistically, call these two different directions 'liberal' idealism and 'conservative' nominalism. Let us illustrate from the experience of the one in whose honour this volume has been compiled.

---

1. It is not our purpose to discuss the theological and philosophical history of the complex question of realism. T. F. Torrance has written an important chapter on some aspects of this matter: 'Theological Realism' (chapter 10) in *The Philosophical Frontiers of Christian Theology: Essays Presented to D. M. MacKinnon*, eds. Brian Hebblethwaite and Stewart Sutherland, Cambridge University Press, 1982.

In 1945, William Still, a young minister of the Church of Scotland, was called to a parish which was not in a thriving condition. Apart from the international problems of the war years and the local problems of Gilcomston South parish, Mr Still began his ministry in a time of notable spiritual decline. The venerable Church of Scotland, and most of her daughter Presbyterian churches throughout the world (not to mention Anglican, Methodist, Lutheran and most others) had long since lost much (though certainly not all) of the original warmth and vitality of their evangelical witness to the grace of God in Christ.

The secularist Enlightenment of the eighteenth century (whose influence on Scottish Christianity has been briefly traced by John MacLeod in *Scottish Theology*, in chapters 7 & 8) and German/British Idealism of the nineteenth century had radically shaken the church's confidence that it could genuinely grasp, know, and offer the eternal Christ and his saving Gospel through the Scriptures to its own generation. In many a pulpit the ideals of the German liberal scholar, Adolph Harnack (famous for reducing Christianity to 'The Father-hood of God, the brotherhood of man, and the infinite value of the human soul'), were substituted for the Christian Gospel of salvation.[2] A vague sort of moralistic do-goodism, shorn of a direct apprehension of God in the Gospel, had emptied (or was in the process of emptying) countless churches in Scotland, England, America and elsewhere.

Behind this 'social gospel' do-goodism (which had lost the Gospel knowledge of God in Christ) lay an important Enlightenment ('liberal' or 'idealist') assumption: finite man cannot know the infinite God through the Scriptures. We cannot survey the historical, theological, and philosophical reasons for and ramifications of this assumption here.[3] Suffice it to say that the vacuum created by a removal of direct knowledge of Christ in the Holy Spirit was inevitably filled with substitutes of many varieties.

In the Protestant world, real union of the believer with Christ in the Holy Spirit tended to be replaced by the ideals, let us say, of German culture, English civilization, American material progress, or (today) by Third World political revolution ('liberation theology'). The common factor in these liberal or idealist variations is ultimately that some form of the human spirit is substituted for the Holy Spirit.

Thus the vitality of the Protestant churches of the western world in general, and much of the Church of Scotland in particular, in the mid 1940's was being sapped at its very roots by a de-supernaturalized, unnatural offspring of evangelical Christianity and secularist idealism. William Still began his ministry in Aberdeen by trumpeting with no uncertain sound the verities of the old, supernatural Gospel with

---

2. Notable Scottish divines of the late 19th and early 20th centuries such as James Denney and James Orr protested against this baneful situation and offered an evangelical alternative.
3. T. F. Torrance would seem to be correct in tracing the root problem to the assumption of a radical disjunction between the intelligible and sensible (or noumenal and phenomenal) worlds. See his article listed in footnote 1.

solemn, yet joyous assurance that men can and must come to know him 'whom to know is life eternal'. He preached that there was no hope in the human spirit, for with all its culture, 'the carnal mind is enmity against God . . .' (Rom. 8:7) and 'the natural man receiveth not the things of the Spirit of God . . .' (1 Cor. 2:14). Regeneration by the Spirit of God is the individual's and the church's only hope: 'Except a man be born again, he cannot see . . . and enter . . . the kingdom of God' (John 3:3, 5). 'No man can come unto me except the Father which hath sent me draw him . . .' (John 6:44).

But the Spirit of God can open eyes to see Christ (John 16:14). God the Father begets us (John 1:12, 13), adopts us (Rom. 8:14-16), implants us in Christ (John chapter 15) and puts Christ in us (Col. 1:27). And it is through 'the foolishness of preaching' (1 Cor. 1:18) by men who, in general, are not wise after the flesh, mighty, or noble (1 Cor. 1:26) that lost sinners come to a genuine saving knowledge of the living God.

Need it be said that for all the glorious results of such a powerful preaching and praying ministry, the realist insistence that through believing the Scriptures one can know the living God in the supernatural atmosphere of the Holy Spirit was — and still is — deeply resented by some both in and out of the Kirk? Why? Perhaps the Roman Catholic scholar, M. Gorce, makes up in clarity and brevity what he lacks in tact when he suggests that the liberal, idealist mind rejects Christian realism (and ultimately all types of realism) simply because it does not want to face squarely the dilemma: 'God or nothing.'[4]

But not only has the Christian church been drawn out of the straight path of knowledge of God by 'liberal' intellectualist idealism, it has also wandered down an equally deadening path of conservative nominalism. Not only would William Still's Aberdeen ministry (and the hundreds of ministries it has spawned) go in a different direction from liberal idealist Christianity, but perhaps surprisingly it has run in a direction quite contrary to some of the major emphases of various forms of conservative evangelicalism.

In his *Work of the Pastor,* Mr Still speaks of the 'conservative' opposition he received after a year and a half in Gilcomston South Church:

> After eighteen months of aggressive evangelism, during which we drew large crowds, mostly of evangelistic folk from every sort of church, assembly, mission and sect, I turned the Word of God upon the Christians for the sake of the large nursery of babes we then had (many of them now grown up), and within a week, from one Sunday to another, you could not see that mission crowd for dust! And they have maligned me all these years for turning from the Gospel, and have even charged me with driving their mollycoddled young people into worldly pleasure halls because I ceased to

4. 'Realisme' by M. Gorce in *Dictionnaire de Theologie Catholique,* Tome 13e, le partie, A. Vacant *et al.* eds., Paris, Librarie Letouzey et Ane, 1936, p. 1875.

provide evangelistic entertainment for them when all I was doing was seeking to feed the lambs.[5]

While we might write off the distaste of the evangelistic enthusiasts for serious expository and prayer-based ministry as chiefly motivated by a desire for 'spiritual entertainment' (in the pre-television days of the '40's), this does not get to the heart of the matter. Not a few evangelicals in the '40's, and not a few today (whether of the Arminian fundamentalist or of Calvinist confessionalist persuasion) — in a sort of reversal of roles with liberal idealism — have used (probably unwittingly) the very Scriptures they strongly profess as an insulation to keep God out of their personal lives. Now we may expect liberals to avoid God (by such obvious tactics as rejecting the authority of Scripture), but how could one seriously suggest that conservatives can also avoid God by means of accepting the Scriptures? Surely, conservative evangelicals would be the greatest realists, for they hold that it is through the Scriptures (and in the Spirit) that one knows God in Christ.

'Yes, but . . .' T. F. Torrance has suggested, with keen insight, that 'ultra-realism' passes over into a type of nominalism. That is, one can so stress the words of the text as being the ultimate truth that one fails to get through them to the living, disturbing Reality of the God who spoke them.[6] One can then re-arrange the words into a particular system of theology, and in so doing avoid some of the less desirable aspects of the truth in its wholeness.

Granted the reality of a devil who ever seeks to unbalance the church from its proper poise on the tightrope of truth, is it unreasonable to suggest that even certain conservatives can use (parts of) Scripture to avoid the uncomfortable Lordship of Christ in their lives? That is, can they not become — instead of strong realists — nominalists (who stress the importance of 'names' — *nomina* — or words, to the exclusion of a higher reality)? Could this, at least in part, explain some of the evangelistic revulsion from the expository, praying ministry established in Aberdeen in 1945?

William Still once commented on this strange phenomenon:

> . . . the most fiendish persecutions have come from evangelistic people who wanted a perpetual preaching of that part of the Gospel which they thought (often wrongly) did not touch them, and who, when the Word of God in its fullness was unleashed upon them, went virtually mad with rage. There is nothing too vile for such people to do when their futile evangelistic round, with its patronage of the unconverted, has been ended, and the myth of their conceited superiority has been destroyed. It takes a man in these circumstances to preach the whole Word of God without fear or favour, whoever it hurts, himself, his loved ones, his friends, or his enemies.[7]

5. William Still, *The Work of the Pastor,* Aberdeen, s.d., — pp. 64, 65.
6. See T. F. Torrance, *Reality and Evangelical Theology,* The Westminster Press, Philadelphia, 1982, pp. 66, 95, 95.
7. W. Still, *ibid.,* pp. 13, 14.

Partial truth will not transform human character until it shines and glows and flames (transfiguration): true truth as far as it goes, which allows carnal, fallen Adamic man of an alien spirit to apply a partial Christ to the old Adam (like giving an old photograph a new face, an old man a new pair of legs, or dressing up an old doll in new supposedly Christian clothes) will not do.[8]

There are two dangers, and we are attacked from two points of view. One, that of being so preoccupied with soundness in the truth, with doctrines, formulations, propositions, and principles, that we go all academic and dead. (Now, surely no one will think I am anti-academic. You come and see how hard I work at scholarship — although I will never be a scholar — and you will soon get that idea out of your head.) The other danger is that we go all activist, constantly running round in fruitless circles, constantly stirring the pot of emotionalism to boiling point, equating the presence and the working of the Spirit with noise, clatter, chatter, laughter and tears, clapping of hands and wringing of hands, etc. In practice it is impossible — I say impossible — for a man to preserve the perfect balance of soundness, and withal spiritual vitality essential to a living ministry, without the poise that comes from the Spirit alone. There is much soundness from which, alas, the Spirit has departed, and soundness soon then becomes rigor mortis. The Spirit departs because the Word must become flesh to confront and challenge and penetrate the minds and hearts, the consciences and wills of other flesh; and men will give any bribe to God to save them becoming power-houses of the Holy Ghost, which they become supremely in preaching. The Word comes alive in men; that's why a life can challenge sometimes without words (although the life that does challenge without words is never without judicious, timely, gracious and searching words).[9]

We must later return to specific ways in which the Gilcomston South ministry radically deviated from what we have termed evangelistic or conservative nominalism.

Facing the deadness of ecclesiastical liberal idealism on the one hand, and the emptiness of para-ecclesiastical conservative and evangelistic nominalism on the other, in the good providence of God, William Still was prepared to pay any price to go straight down the line of historic, supernatural Christian realism. By portraying the William Still-type, expository, praying ministry as a champion of theological realism, we are not of course implying a conscious awareness of the intellectual history of realism, as over against nominalism or idealism. If in 1945 — or 1985 for that matter — one tried to engage Mr Still in a heavy conversation on Platonic universals, Aristotelian class concepts, the Stoic *cataleptic phantasm,* the Alexandrian Patristic doctrine of faith and assent, Thomistic moderate realism, Okhamist nominalism, the Kantian synthetic *apriori,* or Hegelian absolutist idealism, one would stand a good chance of being given short shrift. For instead of worrying with such matters, he would be relentlessly pushing you out into the light of Christ. But if that is not the ultimate in Christian realism, what is?

Mr Still, and the Scottish expository school of ministers who have followed in his train, have devoted themselves to the exercise of a

8. *Ibid.,* p. 93.
9. *Ibid.,* pp. 92, 93.

theologically realist ministry simply because this is the teaching of the Word of God written, and is the time-honoured faith of the true church. The Scriptures are of crucial importance as the inspired Word of God because they lead us up to him who is *The Word of God:*

> And if it is by the written Word alone that we know the authentic, incarnate Word — Christ — then it will never be our duty, or our right, or our licence, to lift Him out of that Word and set Him up as an independent authority, according to our variable predilections. If we do, and separate Christ from His word, try as we may, we will not be able to fashion a Christ who is not in some particular made according to our imperfect image.[10]

> Now consider what this means: the Word of God, the law of God, "the royal law according to the scriptures", "the perfect law of liberty", is a sort of rational, verbal, imprint, transcript, expression, or descriptive mould of the character of God, which character became incarnate and human in Jesus Christ. "He is," says the writer to the Hebrews, "the character, the express image (the matrix, stamp, engraving) of the person or substance of God." (Heb. 1.3). But this written Word, summed up in the incarnate Word, not only expresses what God is like, but is and becomes, by the operation of the Spirit of God, the food, the nourishment by which we become like Him also. To be a pastor of the sheep, a feeder of the Word to others, you must be fed yourself.

> No man can make the Bible become the Word of God (I know that it is, I am not selling you Barth at his worst!) to feed the flock of God by simply passing on what it says. Food has to be assimilated and absorbed by digestion. An atheist could 'teach' the Bible. And some try to — in our schools! That won't do. The Word became flesh, and it must become flesh again in you. It is godly character which is the real pastor — or is the basis of him. You have heard the saying that a man's words could not be heard because what he was and did spoke so loudly. Well, it takes the whole Word of God, impartially received, but rightly divided, to make a rounded, full-orbed character, which every pastor within his God-given limitations must be.[11]

Much of the foundational strength of this growing school of Scottish (and Australian, American, etc.) expository ministry rests in its wholesale commitment to both the absolute authority and the full inspiration of the Holy Scriptures. Its commitment to inspiration safeguards against tendencies toward liberal idealism on the one hand, and on the other hand, its refusal to isolate the words of Scripture from the presence and control of God helps avoid a conservative nominalism which substitutes a humanly manipulated system for the Lordship of Christ.

It is the belief of this writer that the foundational theological balance and the ministerial/sessional methodology and church life that have resulted from the Gilcomston ministry over the last forty years are one of the most important ecclesiastical phenomena of the twentieth century, and can offer substantial guidance and healing to churches which are determined to confront dying men with the eternal life of God in Jesus Christ. For this good reason we must take a look at the

10. W. Still, 'A Charge to Students', in *Theological Students Fellowship Bulletin*, Spring, 1964, pp. 27, 28.
11. W. Still, *Work of the Pastor*, p. 9.

ministerial methodology and corporate prayer of churches such as Gilcomston, which have been prepared to die many deaths to self if only the reality of Jesus Christ in his risen glory can be made known to others (2 Cor. 4:12).

In a word, the whole ministry of these churches is centred in the whole Christ, and to know the whole Christ we need the teaching of the whole Word:

> . . . first, the whole Word, that is to say, the whole truth and nothing but the truth of the whole Bible fed to men in balanced diet. You must learn to be dieticians! I have spent hours discussing the balanced ministry of the Word with other ministers; e.g. what books of the Bible, Old Testament and/or New Testament should follow one another in balanced sequence. The second principle is that the whole Word must be saturated in the living, up-to-date grace of God by His Spirit. If you do not teach the whole Word to your people, both you and they will go astray commensurately to the extent and importance of your omissions; e.g. a Christian needs the book of Proverbs and the epistle of Philemon as well as Genesis, the Psalms, Isaiah, the Gospels, Romans, Galatians, Corinthians, etc.[12]

These words were addressed to newly licensed preachers of the Church of Scotland in Aberdeen in April, 1963 by William Still:

> I charge, you, therefore: preach the Word. Preach the whole Word, however you do it. Whether you do it by following the Church Year . . . or whether you do as some do, preaching through the Bible book by book, chapter by chapter, judiciously alternating Old and New Testaments and different parts of each, the law, the prophets and the writings, the Gospels and Epistles, or whether you do it subject by subject following some scheme of Christian doctrine of the Creeds or Confessions of the church, whatever plan you adopt, preach the whole Word. Do not leave it to chance.[13]

With his realist, Biblical assumption that men can in fact know God directly through the Word in the power of the Spirit, Mr Still and younger colleagues have generally chosen to spend their time actually preaching that Word rather than arguing for the possibility of its being true. Speaking of the loss of Biblical authority in Britain during his lifetime, Mr Still said to a group of ministers at St. Andrews: 'And one has sought with all one's heart and strength to repair that, not so much by presenting strong apologetic arguments for the Bible as the Word of God — that is a field in itself, and this is where I may differ from some of my conservative brothers who have defended the faith ad infinitum rather than declared it, and who have perhaps sometimes unnecessarily antagonised by doing so.' (Church of Scotland In-Service Training Course, September, 1983, p.7). This is to stand with John Calvin, who quoting the great Church Father of the fourth century, Hilary, said: 'For He whom we can know through His own utterances is the best witness concerning Himself.' Those evangelicals who are spending their whole time debating endlessly among themselves the merits and demerits of evidential versus presuppositional apologetics might do

12. *Ibid.,* pp. 57, 58.
13. W. Still, 'A Charge to Students', pp. 29, 30.

well to heed these words, and begin preaching the Gospel they defend
to the lost whom they assert need it.

The determination to preach the whole Word in all of its parts with
all of its demands and promises is simply a modern application of the
old Puritan Regulative Principle.[14] And like Puritanism at its best, the
modern Scottish expository ministry is interested in preaching of (and
regulation by) the whole Word because that is the way the Spirit of
Christ takes on flesh and blood in the lives of his people.

> You must not live in the world of books, but in the world of men. Yet, all
> that is worth saying to men of lasting value comes from books. But it is all
> summed up in a Man; and the end is never propositions, theories,
> precepts, doctrines, but a certain kind of flesh and blood. The Word
> became Man to be man, in you and me, for ever. God will never cease to
> be Man. He is a Man for ever.[15]
> Indeed, my whole view of the Christian's responsibility for primary
> evangelism is founded upon the belief that the greatest evangelistic and
> pastoral agency in the world is the Holy Spirit dwelling naturally in God's
> children, so that Christ shines out of them all the time or nearly all the
> time, and is known to do so by those with whom they have anything more
> than casual contact — and even with them.[16]

Another strength of the Scottish expository ministry is the realistic
— and hopeful — way it faces the high cost of letting the whole Christ
through the whole Word loose in our whole lives.

> One last word: the whole current of the divine electricity has to pass
> through you, His servant, and little though you may know what is going on
> in the hearts of your people at first, there is a great price to be paid for
> being the conductor of divine truth and power. Change the figure: this is
> dynamite, and you will have to die to explode its truth in human hearts,
> and will have to go down into a new death every time you bring forth God's
> living Word to the people (2 Cor. 4:12). You will have to die, not only to
> your own sin, but to self in many of its most seemingly innocent and
> legitimate aspects, for only then can the death and resurrection power of
> Jesus Christ be communicated to men, and you dare not do less for any
> people than this. If you do less, you will have to answer before God one
> day.[17]
> If we are not prepared to suffer (and suffering is not fun and is not meant to
> be fun), we shall not reign. The two belong together, as Peter says over
> and over again in his first epistle. Hurt and fruit, death and life, sorrow and
> joy, they belong together, as manure belongs to a fruitful garden.[18]

To let the whole Word loose in our personalities, that is, to bow low
to the universal lordship of Christ over us and over all that is ours,
requires nothing less than radical surgery upon the self-life. And
appropriate surgery can at times be absolutely essential to good health.
In our opinion this kind of radical surgery must be performed on some
segments of the evangelistic church today in order to restore it to

---

14. On the Regulative Principle, see Iain Murray, ed., *The Reformation of the Church,* Banner of
Truth Trust, London, 1965, pp. 37-50.
15. W. Still, *The Work of the Pastor,* p. 81.
16. *Ibid.,* pp. 35,36.
17. *Ibid.,* p. 21.
18. *Ibid.,* p. 79.

soundness of health. To give a specific example, some groups of evangelistic Christians in the United States are caught up in a kind of magical nominalism which requires the cutting work of a realistic scapula upon it.

These evangelists, some of whom are well known on television and radio, emphasize *prosperity* in their teaching. They teach that if you exercise faith properly you will be at all times blessed with health and wealth. The key to gaining health and wealth is called 'naming and claiming'. That is, if you begin saying the words 'I am going to get a better paying job', those words (uttered in Christ's name, of course) will turn into physical reality. This is sheer nominalism, if not magic. The words (for instance, some promise of Scripture about material blessing for God's people) are cut off from their referent in the Person, purposes, and glory of God, and then are manipulated to accomplish the purposes and glory of man. The only hope is to attempt to stab these people awake from their materialist dream-world by pointing them to the excelling glory of co-crucifixion and co-resurrection with Christ (Romans 6), 'by whom we are crucified to the world and the world to us' (Gal. 6:14), and with whom God 'hath raised us up together, and made us sit together in heavenly places in Christ Jesus' (Ephesians 2:6). The theological realism of an expository, obedient, praying ministry is the only scapula that can accomplish such an operation.

The realist knife of the whole Word performed surgery not only upon the individual believer under the ministry of William Still, but upon the entire structure and procedure of the church. All sorts of extra meetings and ecclesiastical organizations were cut out in order to make room for the great realities which would render those lesser concerns unnecessary. With the Word being searchingly preached three times a week as well as the intercessory prayer meeting on Saturday nights, God was doing his work and various clubs and drives were no longer needed nor even appropriate in light of the glory that was excelling such things. In addition to this change, children were now expected to be brought into the regular preaching and prayer services so that separate youth activities (beyond Sunday School for the smallest children) were excised. The constant question put to all of these things was this: 'What is the end of our activities?' What can this meeting or organization do for the transformation of life to the glory of God that the preaching of the Word and praying could not do better?

The integration of children into the regular life of the church at worship was to have important implications for the ministry later in their lives. This meant the cutting out of panicky, evangelistic gimmicks in favour of a more realistic view of human psychology and spiritual development:

> Every autumn I have a spate of letters from fond parents, teachers, guardians, and monitors, appealing to me to follow up such-and-such a

youngster who is away from home at College for the first time, and who has to be hunted, followed, shadowed, intercepted and driven to Christian meetings. I have scarcely ever known this desperate technique to work. I understand the panic of parents and guardians, but it is too late then to try high pressure tactics. Prayer, example, and precept, in that order, are the means of bringing children and young folk up in the faith; nor will high-pressure tactics and brain-washing techniques avail when young folk have gone off on their own. Some young folk, alas, will have their fling, and some sow their wild oats and come at last to heel sadly, like the prodigal son. It is where Christians pathetically put their trust in external techniques and artificial stratagems that young folk go astray. Nothing takes the place of the realism of holy living and secret wrestling before God in prayer for our youngsters. We must commit them to God so utterly that we dare not interfere or tamper with their precious souls.[19]

Another area where a tendency to gimmickry was purposely rejected to make room for a realistic relationship to God was in the matter of evangelism in the church. In the post-Finney and Moody Protestant evangelical world, the innovation of asking people to walk the aisle to register public acceptance of Christ as Lord and Saviour has at times (though certainly not always) tended to degenerate into another sort of nominalism, which has been termed by some 'decisional regeneration'. The implication is that if one goes through the public action of coming forward and saying the words then one is assured of regeneration. Though those who think this way have never heard the term, theirs is a kind of nominalism in which Biblical phrases and human responses can be cut off from the sovereign and mysterious power of the Living God, whose Spirit is like the wind: 'The wind bloweth where it wills, and thou hearest the sound thereof, but canst not tell whence it cometh, and whither it goeth: so is every one that is born of the Spirit' (John 3:8).

In place of a constant pressure to respond to an invitation at the end of a service (with the implied promise that human response will guarantee divine regeneration), the Scottish expository ministry is pointing the way to a far more Biblical and healthy — that is, realistic — approach to soul winning and edification. The Revd James Philip has written on this matter as follows:

The Apostle's evangelism was teaching evangelism. It is misleading to identify 'preaching the Gospel' with 'preaching an evangelistic message'. All the evidence of the New Testament goes to show that the Apostle's evangelism was a teaching evangelism. All the character messages in Acts have the kerygma (proclamation about Christ) at their heart — it was doctrinal preaching all the time, based on the Scriptures, expounding and interpreting them. 'Paul, as his manner was, reasoned, or argued, with them out of the Scriptures, opening and alleging . . .' (Acts 17:2, 3). Rightly understood, apostolic evangelism is not a matter of exhorting and pressing men to come to Christ until there has been a proclamation of the mighty acts of God in Christ in reconciliation and redemption, and on the basis of this, the free offer of His Grace is made to all who will receive it.[20]

19. *Ibid.*, p. 39.
20. James Philip in *The Work of the Pastor* by W. Still, pp. 5,6.

Mr Still adds:

> It follows therefore that the Church's evangelism ought to be one in which all the counsel of God is made known to men. We need a recovery of belief in the converting and sanctifying power of the living Word of God in the teaching of the pulpit, and its ability to transform the lives of men and produce in them the lineaments and fruits of mature Christian character.[21]

What this means methodologically is that evangelism is not best carried out by holding an annual series of meetings in which one preaches on certain Gospel texts and urges men to decision (although in particular times and places this may be entirely appropriate). On the contrary, the truest, deepest evangelism is carried out in the non-dramatic, regular course of preaching through the various books of Scripture in the week-by-week, consistent ministry of the local church — Sunday morning and evening, and Wednesday night: especially as this teaching is 'oiled' and 'set on fire' through the prayers of believers reaching the throne of God in both concerted and individual effort. This is precisely what Christian theological realism means when applied to the realm of practical methodology in the church.

As we noted at the beginning of this chapter, the ultimate concern of Christian theological realism is that men come face to face with the Living God. Those who know God best are those who pray most. If B. B. Warfield of Princeton was right in defining Calvinism as 'religion on its knees before God in prayer', then nowhere is true Calvinism flourishing more than in the Gilcomston-inspired expository, praying ministries. From beginning to end, the Saturday night intercessory prayer meeting has been constantly stressed as absolutely essential to the accomplishment of the purposes of God in the life of the congregation and of the world at large. These prayer meetings have a way of keeping the people in a posture of dependence on God and self-abandonment. They will not allow one to stop short of anything less than coming into actual contact with the grace and glory of God. The multifarious forms of man-centred nominalism and gimmickry wither away, under the reality of the Triune God inspiring and then answering the prayers of his people.

We must mention one final result of the Christian realism of the Scottish expository ministry: its high view of the corporate church. Here again, it can serve as a healthy corrective to modern Protestant evangelical forms of the individualistic, atomistic nominalism that was so destructive to the Catholic synthesis in the late Medieval period. To put it simply, some strands in Medieval nominalism denied the reality of class concepts and corporate life, and put all emphasis on isolated individuals with a consequent denial of the reality and importance of relationship. A not dissimilar, post-Renaissance form of isolated individualism has plagued the Protestant churches for centuries, and

---

21. William Still, *The Work of the Pastor*, p. 6.

perhaps has been at its strongest among evangelicals.

In face of this separateness, William Still and others have re-emphasized the importance of corporate prayer, corporate worship, and the covenant concept of child rearing. Furthermore, they have perceived that numerous 19th and 20th century para-ecclesiastical organizations sprang up because the church was failing to do what it was supposed to do in ministering the Word and corporately praying. As the church once again lays lesser things aside in order to return to its true task, many of these organizations can gracefully fade into the background as the body of Christ is re-invigorated to perform its varied ministries in the world (which it lost by default to other organizations).

Not all evangelicals will agree with William Still's belief that one should remain within a theologically mixed denomination until one is put out,[22] but none can deny the value of his high view of the church as the living body of Christ in a lost and dying world. But owing to the Biblical balance of his Christian realist position, he does not put the church, nor its doctrinal confession (for all its value), between the needy soul and the God of grace. On the contrary, the Scottish expository ministry which he has in some measure inspired is a fresh and powerful witness that Word, sacraments, and confession are no more and no less than means of grace: open doors through which the God of all grace meets his people, transforms their lives, changes their culture, and glorifies his Son.

22. *Ibid.*, p. 99.

THE PULPIT BIBLE:

Preaching and the Logic of Authority

NIGEL M. de S. CAMERON

William Still, for whom we give thanks to Almighty God and to whom we gladly pay tribute in these pages, is before anything else a preacher. His contributions to the life and thought of the Church have been many, but it is his practice and encouragement of expository preaching that have singled him out and given him such influence, both in Scotland and (as this volume demonstrates) much further afield.

Yet he is not a preacher *simpliciter*, he is a preacher of the Word. The content and the manner of his preaching are reflections of his preoccupation with the Holy Scriptures. The ministry of William Still therefore raises in a form that is acute a question which has long lain behind the church's use of Scripture.

The Crisis of Authority

The question of the authority of the Bible has been at the centre of the crisis of belief which has enveloped the church for more than a century, since that which holds the most central place in the practice of the Church's faith has become the object of the most serious doubt. The early Christians inherited from their Jewish forebears a belief in Holy Scripture as the Word of God. For them this first referred to the Old Testament, but soon also to the writings of the New, as is already evident in II Peter 3: 15, 16 where (some of) the Apostle Paul's writings are treated as on a par with the 'other' Scriptures.

Scripture as the Word of God was understood to have plenary authority. That is to say, it had authority on any subject on which it touched. This authority served a two-fold function, which we may depict as *doctrinal* and *practical*. It is evident already in the use made of the Old Testament by the writers of the New. *Doctrinally* the role of Scripture was to define the faith, and *practically* it was to serve as the authority for the preaching of the faith: both to instruct those who believed it already, and to commend it to those who did not.

Both these uses of Holy Scripture to authenticate theological statements continue to this day, whether such statements are intended to *define* the faith (as in the formulation of doctrinal standards) or to *teach* and *commend* it (as in the tradition of preaching which lies at the heart of our Reformed worship).

But these uses of Scripture have continued without regard to the fundamentally new way in which the Bible has come to be viewed by the majority of Protestant Christians.[1] Conservative evangelicals claim that they are almost alone within the Protestant Churches today in holding to the plenary authority of Holy Scripture, a belief which was once universal in the Church, and it is hard to see how either element in this claim can be gainsaid. Striking testimony has been borne to it by Kirsopp Lake, the famous New Testament scholar who found himself at the opposite end of the spectrum from the conservatives in the 'Fundamentalist' controversy in the United States during the early part of this century. Lake wrote as follows:

> It is a mistake, often made by educated men who happen to have but little knowledge of historical theology, to suppose that Fundamentalism is a new and strange form of thought. It is nothing of the kind: it is the partial and uneducated survival of a theology that was once universally held by all Christians. How many were there, for instance, in the Christian Churches, in the eighteenth century, who doubted the infallible inspiration of all Scripture? A few, perhaps, but very few. No, the Fundamentalist may be wrong; I think he is. But it is we who have departed from the tradition, not he, and I am sorry for anyone who tries to argue with a Fundamentalist on the basis of authority. The Bible, and the *corpus theologicum* of the Church, is [*sic*] on the Fundamentalist side.[2]

No doubt Lake's case could be disputed in some particulars. It would certainly need to be qualified, not least in his assertion that the conservative evangelicalism, as we should call it, of the early years of this century was 'uneducated'. The conservative ranks included such distinguished scholars as B. B. Warfield and J. Gresham Machen; and, as his comments themselves imply, there were 'uneducated' liberals too! Lake's essential proposition, that the conservatives of his day were defending the tradition of the historic church, is difficult to contest. Theological conservatives today accept the mantle Lake offered. In Christian doctrine in general, and in the doctrine of Holy Scripture in particular, they bear the standard of the historic Church's understanding of Holy Scripture.

But what of the adequacy of alternative concepts of Scripture for the functions which Scripture is still called on to perform, as much by those who deny its plenary authority as by those who accept it? This question is raised because, despite the fact that widespread scepticism as to the truthfulness of Scripture (historical/factual, even theological/ethical) has dominated Protestant theological endeavour for a century and more, when the Bible is being *used* rather than *examined* it is largely allowed to play the roles it has always played.[3] And that is so whether it

1. The position in the Roman Catholic church is, of course, markedly different, with a strong tradition of conservative Biblical interpretation which is largely parallel to that which has been maintained within Protestant churches almost exclusively by conservative evangelicals. See the fascinating pair of essays by J. I. Packer and S. B. Clark in *Christianity Confronts Modernity*, edited by P. Williamson and K. Perrotta, Edinburgh 1981.
2. Kirsopp Lake, *The Religion of Yesterday and Tomorrow*, London, 1925, pp. 61, 2.
3. As one distinguished theologian remarked to the present writer during discussion of the authority of Scripture, 'people only say they aren't Fundamentalists when they're asked'. He was not one himself.

is being called upon to define and justify doctrinal proposals in a formal context (with an updated version of the old 'proof text') or to authenticate them in the context of preaching and teaching.[4]

It is at this point that everyone associated with the Church (whether as member or adherent, joining in public worship, Bible class or Sunday School) is confronted with the practical question of the authority of Scripture, since they find themselves recipients of the teaching of Christian doctrine and ethics that is founded upon, and generally *claimed* to be founded upon, the authority of the Bible. Yet it is a Bible whose authority the majority of those engaged in such teaching accept only selectively. They would themselves deny that their disbelief in this or that element in the Bible prejudiced the propriety of their use of those elements in it which they choose to accept. Of course: a failure to make such a claim would involve an admission of fundamental inconsistency. The question remains whether the rejection of the authority of Scripture in particular areas does not entail the rejection of its authority as a whole. That is to say, in those areas in which its teaching is accepted, is it accepted because of the authority of Scripture, or is it accepted because in these particular cases the teaching of Scripture happens to coincide with positions taken up for other reasons?

The most consistent feature of contemporary avowals and denials of Biblical authority is their idiosyncratic character. This needs to be emphasised, since many who have somewhat unreflectingly adopted what they take to be the orthodoxy of the day believe that they have taken up a single and consistent alternative to the orthodoxy of an earlier day (which they may or may not recognise with the candour of Kirsopp Lake to be *the* orthodoxy of the Christian tradition). That is to say, they are under the impression that there is no necessity to believe the Bible to possess plenary authority since its authority is independent of any such formulation; and since most modern Christian thinkers and preachers have moved from it to an eclectic alternative.

But *there is no such single 'alternative'*. What alone is common to 'alternative' notions of Biblical authority is their denial that authority is plenary. That is, they are united in denying the belief of an earlier day that the teaching of Scripture is authoritative on whatever it touches; but they deny it in different places and for different reasons. They have no consensus alternative to set in its stead. In the context of the north American debate to which we have already made reference, B. B. Warfield of Princeton assessed the position in these words:

4. Which is not to go into the question of whether there is an essential difference between preaching and teaching, in the context of the Christian congregation. The present writer's view is that the difference is one of emphasis rather than kind, but that it can be great enough for a distinction to be made for practical purposes. For the present discussion it is enough to state that all Christian preaching and teaching contains an irreducible element of doctrinal and/or ethical content which must somehow be justified, and which is in fact justified (candidly or covertly) by appeal to Holy Scripture.

> The old formula, *quot homines tot sententiae*, seems no longer adequate. Wherever five "advanced thinkers" assemble, at least six theories as to inspiration are likely to be ventilated. They differ in every conceivable point, or in every conceivable point save one. They agree that inspiration is less pervasive and less determinative than has heretofore been thought, or than is still thought in less enlightened circles. They agree that there is less of the truth of God and more of the error of man in the Bible than Christians have been wont to believe. They agree accordingly that the teaching of the Bible may be, in this, that or the other, — here, there or elsewhere, — safely neglected or openly repudiated. So soon as we turn to the constructive side, however, and ask wherein the inspiration of the Bible consists; how far it guarantees the trustworthiness of the Bible's teaching; in what of its elements is the Bible a divinely safeguarded guide to truth: the concurrence ends and hopeless dissension sets in. They agree only in their common destructive attitude towards some higher view of the inspiration of the Bible, of the presence of which each one seems supremely conscious.[5]

If, as we would suggest, this is as true today as it was when it was first penned, it is incumbent upon those who dissent from the historic doctrine of Biblical authority to explain the logic of their position. In particular, they must be able to explain how their own doubts about the Bible relate to the confidence which they invite others to have in it at points where they accept its teaching, which they desire to commend. It is a question which affects every minister as he prepares for his pulpit ministry, and as he addresses his congregation with an open Bible before him. Indeed, it affects him at least as much when he, or someone in his place, reads from the Scriptures before he preaches, because the reading of Scripture in the context of public worship is presumptive of its authority before ever the preacher begins to cite its propositions in justification of his message to the people.

Is the preaching and public reading of the Holy Scriptures any longer justified, in a theological context in which some or many of the statements of Scripture are denied? What, may we ask, is the logical force of an appeal to an authority which is partly authoritative and partly not, unless there is an indisputably clear criterion which will determine how statements of the one kind are to be distinguished from statements of the other? After more than a century, this remains a question which has never been satisfactorily answered. It is generally ignored.

Authority in Question

There are several ways in which the *prima facie* authority of Scripture has been called into question. We cannot here attempt a systematic assessment of them. But we can survey some typical ways in which those who reject the tradition seek to set aside statements in Scripture with which they do not agree. In each instance what we note is that, even within a single area, it is unusual for there to be

---

5. 'The Inspiration of the Bible', in *The Works of Benjamin B. Warfield,* 10 vols, OUP, New York, 1927, reprinted 1981, i, p. 51.

consistency; that is to say, those who generally reject material in a given area will still wish to retain *some* claims for Biblical authority within this area, while repudiating others.

We take four areas in which doubt as to the authority of the teaching of Scripture has led to attempts to reconstruct an idea of Biblical authority which can survive doubt and, indeed, disbelief. The first concerns *historical* claims in Scripture, the second elements of the *miraculous*, the third *ethical* or *practical* injunctions, and the fourth *doctrinal* assertions. Plainly there is overlap between these areas; that, indeed, is one of the main features which emerges in the discussion which follows, and one of the chief difficulties which modern attempts to reconstruct the idea of Biblical authority must face.

It is at first sight a simple matter to decide that, since the subject-matter of the revelation of God is religious, the historical statements in Scripture can be left open to doubt while the theological statements are believed. There are certainly very many people who think so. The problem with this approach is two-fold. First, as we have noted, such a view will invariably be held alongside a conviction of the major importance of *some* historical events recorded in Scripture, which (it will be said) are not in doubt, while *others* are rejected.

This seems at first blush to be deeply inconsistent, and on further examination the seeming inconsistency does not disappear, but rather demonstrates that the criterion of selection actually at work is not what is claimed. Some historical events are to be rejected, others are fundamentally important and cannot be doubted. But the grounds on which one Biblical event is doubted must be allowed to operate in relation to other Biblical events. If, let us say, the Biblical narrative of the fall of Jericho is held to be doubtful on the grounds of general historical enquiry, then in principle every Biblical event must be open to doubt, and even those for which there is good general historical evidence can never be taken as foundations for faith, since all historical evidence is a matter of probabilities. We believe the Biblical history *either* because it is the Biblical history, *or* because the secular historian warrants that it is, at a given point, after all the available evidence has been weighed, probably reliable. We may not reasonably decide to believe *a* happened for the first reason (the Bible tells us) while at the same time doubting whether *b* happened for the second (the historian thinks it is in some degree unlikely).

Which leads us to the second aspect of the problem which this approach faces. Certain Biblical events are held to be crucial, even if only the major elements in the life of Jesus Christ, since (it is said) their historical character, while generally considered necessary, is secondary to their theological significance. But what of other *prima facie* historical events? Do they not also partake of a *theological*, as opposed to a merely *historical*, importance? A special problem arises with an event like the Exodus from Egypt, which is foundational for the entire theological structure of the Old Testament and therefore of the New.

If there had been no Exodus (and there are many scholars who would doubt whether anything like it ever took place) it does not raise merely historical, but fundamental theological, difficulties. Yet it is merely a special case of a general problem. What we are presented with in the Holy Scriptures is, as we might say, a religion in the guise of a history. There is nothing 'merely historical' in the Bible, and while (of course) it would be foolish to pretend that there are no events recorded which are of very minor significance, it would be more foolish still to pretend that even they were of no significance whatever. In principle the entire record is of religious-theological importance.

A second approach would focus on the miraculous element in Scripture as something (at least, in some measure) beyond belief. The Gospel miracles form a major portion of the miraculous material in Scripture. There are those who accept them while disbelieving miraculous accounts in the Old Testament, while others would seek naturalistic explanations for the Gospel stories which, they would suggest, were the result of misunderstanding or exaggeration (so that, in a classic instance, the feeding of the five thousand was generated by the crowd's response to the boy's generosity: he shared his picnic, so they did too).

The essential ground for rejecting miraculous accounts in Scripture is a naturalistic approach to historical events. This is a reasonable approach, or so it seems, in that we have only our experience of the present to use as a guide to the past. What is credible in Scripture is what we would expect today. Yet the problem with this approach is that it proves too much. Such an assessment of the Biblical narrative would excise *every* miraculous element, including the plainest miracle of all, the incarnation of Jesus Christ.

But the difficulty goes deeper, for the miraculous element in Scripture is not confined to this miracle or that; not even to the great miracle of the incarnation, with its culmination in the resurrection of Jesus Christ. Any religion of revelation is inherently and fundamentally miraculous. That is to say, it is impossible to receive the Biblical religion as anything other than one extended miracle, inexplicable in its entirety as a merely natural phenomenon. During the nineteenth century there were systematic attempts to re-write the Biblical history to make it accord with the evolutionary naturalism of the day. Such an approach must either prove too thorough-going for even its supporters (resulting in a scaling-down of the faith of the Bible to the consequence of human insight and endeavour) or, as has tended to be the result, it has had to draw back from its declared intention, and qualify its method in order to make room for the Biblical religion; and so admitted its arbitrary character.

A third approach would seek to reject aspects of the ethical and practical teaching of the Scriptures. Since this can raise complex issues concerning the relation of the testaments, we confine our discussion to New Testament teaching. In, for example, the controversy about the place of women in the Church, or in the family, some would argue that the New Testament writers have been misinterpreted; that they do not intend to say what they seem to say. Others, while accepting that the Apostle Paul teaches that women should be subordinate to their husbands, and that they should not occupy certain roles within the Church, reject the relevance of his teaching for the Church of today. This latter kind of argument represents a rejection of the normative character of Biblical ethical injunctions, since (in the instances we have cited) we read fundamental theological arguments used in support of the Apostle's contentions, not arguments *ad hominem* or addressed to special situations.

The difficulty here, once again, is that the interpreter is without an objective criterion by which to choose when he is to accept and when to reject an ethical injunction. Another, striking, example is that of homosexual behaviour, plainly condemned in the New Testament. If it is open to us to reject that condemnation, what of the condemnation of fornication and of adultery? May we not, with as much or as little justification, decide to reject such prohibitions too?

Our fourth category, that of doctrine, raises analogous, if more fundamental, problems. It is remarkable that ill-considered repudiations of Biblical authority so frequently resolve into objections to Biblical doctrine, since this is the element to which lip-service is most generally paid. Indeed the close connection of each of the three foregoing with this most fundamental category is revealed by the way in which objections to history, miracle and ethical injunctions in Scripture are in fact deeper-rooted. The fundamental doctrine which proves to be at stake is the doctrine of God, since aspects of the Biblical revelation of the character of God are found to be unpalatable and are, in consequence, repudiated as lacking authority for the church today.

Thus records of the acts of God may be held to be unhistorical partly because they are miraculous and therefore incredible (such as the plagues and drowning of Pharoah recorded in Exodus), and partly also because God is conceived by the modern interpreter as not 'being like that'. He *could* not have done what is attributed to him; so he did not do it; so it did not happen. Whereas another miraculous account (let us say the resurrection), while *prima facie* equally improbable and historically unprovable is accepted, since it represents the sort of thing which God might be expected to do. In this case a preconceived idea of the character of God, formed by a selective induction of the Biblical material, is employed to reject other elements in that material and so make the whole conform to the interpreter's image.

A similar approach is seen in some responses to the ethical injunctions forbidding the practice of homosexuality. Since the notion of a God who forbids and who judges is alien to the modern interpreter, evidence that the God of the Bible does indeed forbid and judge is excised. The ill-informed approach of so many people to the Biblical teaching on the subject of eternal punishment furnishes a straightforward example, in that the teaching is undeniably present. It is common to hear it said that this doctrine conflicts with the teaching of Jesus, and for it to be blamed on the Old Testament or the distorting effects of the Apostle Paul on the Christian faith. In fact, were it not for the teaching of Jesus on the subject we should have very limited material on which to build *any* Biblical doctrine of eternal punishment. It is, of all the doctrines taught in Holy Scripture, the most distinctively dominical.

But this fourth example, in which the authority of Scripture in explicitly doctrinal matters is held to be less than absolute, reveals most plainly the arbitrary character of interpretation of this kind. It functions by comparing the doctrines taught in Scripture with some prior concept of (for example) the character of God, and accepting or rejecting those doctrines according to their conformity or lack of conformity to that concept. Plainly this is no acceptance of Biblical authority, it is the elevation of the preconceptions of the interpreter over the Bible, in such a way as to ensure that the Bible itself is brought into conformity with the interpreter's own position.

The Pulpit Use of Scripture

We would therefore suggest that modern interpreters have failed to establish an acceptable criterion by which what is authoritative may be distinguished from what is not in the sacred text. On the contrary, there is a fatally subjective and arbitrary element in all Biblical interpretation which rejects the plenary authority of Scripture.

But this is especially evident when we consider the task of the preacher. He generally adopts, for didactic purposes, the traditional preaching form of the exposition of Holy Scripture, standing in the tradition of the ancient as well as the Reformation church. Yet the consensus theological tradition of the day repudiates the major premise of such a didactic use of Scripture, denying plenary authority to the canon of the church. The fundamental illogic of every doctrinal formulation which *argues from Scripture while denying to Scripture, in effect, any right to be argued from*, is repeated in every sermon which begins with a text but will not allow comparable authority to other such texts. The major premise of the pulpit use of Holy Scripture is its plenary authority, yet, like the smile of the Cheshire cat, the pulpit usage remains long after the cat has vanished. Only those who have broken radically and self-consciously with the Christian tradition (such as the Unitarians, who may be found with a string quartet in the place of the sermon at public worship; and individual radicals within the major denominations) have abandoned the old *form* of preaching as didactic instruction out of the Scriptures. At the same time, many who maintain the old form have so far emptied it of its content (in taking a 'text' as a mere *bon mot* with which to introduce their own, independent, reflections) as to deny it any serious influence on what is held to follow. Yet the pattern remains: reading, text, preaching, with its assumption of a logic in which an authority attaches to the preaching which is not merely that of the preacher, but that of his text — and, therefore, of its author, who is God.

The passage which functions as a 'text' is typically brief, and the practice of employing a 'text' for developing an argument which is independent of what it says depends upon such brevity. But the 'text' can also be a longer passage, and the fuller the 'text' the more difficult it is for the preacher to abuse it (by accident or design), since what it says will be generally plainer and more difficult to misinterpret or ignore. It is interesting that the revival of expository preaching with which William Still's name is particularly associated does not follow the 'text-preaching' of earlier evangelical preachers, but more normally takes much longer passages as 'texts' such as Calvin took in his Sermons. Following him, William Still has worked his way steadily through all the books of the Old and New Testaments. Yet, as he would readily admit, there is no necessary relationship between this form and the content which it is intended to convey. It would be possible, if unlikely, for an interpreter who rejected the plenary authority of Scripture to twist it systematically to conform to his own preconceptions of religious truth. It is more likely that he would use another method. And other methods may equally be employed to this end, to bring to bear the teaching of Holy Scripture: preaching from texts, from the clauses of the great creeds, from the chapters of the confessions of the Reformation, from the seasons of the Christian Year — to draw out the teaching of Scripture and present it for the edification and challenge of the congregation; and it is to this task that the preacher is called.

And, as he fulfils his calling, expounding the 'Word of God written' (as it is called in the *XXXIX Articles*) he bears unwitting testimony to the plenary authority of the Word by which, through his Holy Spirit, God speaks today as he has in every day.

> A glory gilds the sacred page,
> Majestic, like the sun;
> It gives a light to every age;
> It gives, but borrows none.

WORD, MINISTRY AND CONGREGATION IN THE REFORMATION CONFESSIONS

DAVID F. WRIGHT

The ministry of William Still has been distinguished by a grand simplification of the work of the ministry, in the conviction that the two main weapons the Lord has given to his Church are preaching and praying. Central to the growing evangelical movement in the Church of Scotland which honours him as its senior father-in-God is a similar persuasion that the minister's calling is above all to be an expositor of the Word and to lead the congregation in prayer, and to sit loose to many other activities that 'the ministry' has accumulated over the generations.

The Reformation of the sixteenth century was likewise characterized by a drastic simplification of Christianity. The burdensome paraphernalia of medieval Catholicism were dumped by the cartload (sometimes quite literally), and the faith reformed assumed a leaner, stripped-down profile — in theology, in Church government, in Christian piety, in worship, in Church buildings, in ecclesiastical law, indeed in almost every area of the Church's life. It seems appropriate, therefore, in a volume that pays tribute to an outstandingly faithful minister of Christ and his Church, to examine how the Reformation confessions present the reformed ministry. The confessions alone cannot be expected to yield a comprehensive picture of Reformation approaches to the ministry; for this one would need to quarry much more widely. Nevertheless, it should be instructive to discover, from those texts which most deliberately set forth for public consumption the fundamental teachings of the Christian faith as the Reformation Churches recognized them, how the ministry was understood — in other words, what they felt they must *confess* about the ministry.

A further justification may be cited for questioning the confessions about the ministry. Some of them are a direct reflection of preaching and teaching ministries in reformed Churches, or apologiae for those ministries. The Augsburg Confession of 1530, the standard-bearer of all the Reformation confessions and still the basic confession of the Lutheran Churches, is presented by its signatories as 'a confession of our pastors' and preachers' teaching and of our own faith, setting forth how and in what manner, on the basis of the Holy Scriptures, these things are preached, taught, communicated and embraced in our lands' (Preface). Its several articles are nearly all introduced by 'Our Churches teach' or 'It is also taught among us'. This stance is no less marked in the Tetrapolitan Confession which was drawn up for presentation to the same imperial Diet of Augsburg on behalf of four cities, led by Strasbourg, which could not endorse the Augsburg Confession, especially on the Lord's Supper. Its first section is entitled 'Of the Subject-Matter of Sermons', declaring that 'our preachers' have been enjoined 'to teach from the pulpit nothing else than is either contained in the Holy Scriptures or has sure ground therein'. Thereafter reference is repeatedly made to the principled practice of 'our preachers' or 'our churchmen'.

Not all sixteenth-century confessions claim to be such direct transcripts of their Churches' preaching activity, but the apologetic, 'Here-we-stand' posture is often no less clearly expressed. The Preface to the Scots Confession (1560) laments that no earlier opportunity has availed to make 'known to the world the doctrine which we profess and for which we have suffered abuse and danger'. Its articles begin with 'we acknowledge, confess, believe' rather than with verbs of preaching and teaching. The Gallican (French) Confession of 1559 is prefaced by an appeal to King Francis II pleading for relief from the persecutions experienced by French Protestants for adhering to the doctrines set out in the Confession.

Confessions like these may claim a degree of continuity with the primitive Christian tradition which linked confession closely with martyrdom, and indeed with the One who bore a good confession before Pontius Pilate (1 Tim. 6:13). Perhaps confessions should always give clear evidence of the readiness to suffer, if not the actual experience of suffering, for the faith confessed. Their theology should certainly be kerygmatic — not only preachable but already proved in the crucible of preaching. Viewed in this light confessions are as much the work of preachers as of theologians.

Church and Ministry

If one were to feel justified, in such a study, in turning first to the Westminster Confession, one would find with surprise that it assigns no chapter to the ministry of the Church, despite having chapters not only on the Church and the sacraments, but also on Church Censures and Synods and Councils. The explanation may partly lie in the fact that the Westminster Assembly produced also the Form of Presbyterial Church Government and the Directory of Public Worship, both of which are almost wholly taken up with the ordering and duties of ministers. But this circumstance cannot of itself account for the Confession's lack of a separate statement on the ministry, since the Directory deals with other topics, such as Baptism, the Lord's Supper and the Sanctification of the Lord's Day, which the Confession also covers. It is, in fact, in the chapters on these and related subjects that the Confession's doctrine of ministry, such as it is, may be found.

'The ministry of the Word' is assumed by the chapter on Effectual Calling (10:3, 4) and more specifically by the one on Religious

Worship and the Sabbath-Day (21:5). The nearest thing to a formal articulation of a doctrine of ministry appears in the Confession's statement on the Church. To the visible, catholic Church 'Christ has given the ministry, oracles, and ordinances of God, for the gathering and perfecting of the saints in this life' (25:3). The purity of particular Churches (which are members of this universal Church) is commensurate with the purity with which 'the doctrine of the gospel is taught and embraced, ordinances administered and public worship performed ... in them' (25:4). Further references to Christ's appointment of ministers are contained in the chapters on the Lord's Supper and on Church Censures.

Ministry, then, can hardly be judged one of the Westminster Confession's strong points. Nevertheless, the way it speaks of ministry illustrates an important theological principle, that the doctrine of ministry belongs under the doctrine of the Church and not vice-versa. This is borne out in many of the sixteenth-century confessions, which introduce the ministry in the context of identifying the true Church of Christ. The Anglican Thirty-Nine Articles (1563/1571) declare the Church to be 'a congregation of faithful men in which the pure Word of God is preached and the sacraments be duly ministered according to Christ's ordinance' (19). In the Augsburg Confession the Church is presented as 'the assembly of all believers among whom the gospel is preached in its purity and the holy sacraments are administered according to the gospel' (7), although we should note that it has already spoken of 'the office of the ministry' as the God-given means of obtaining the faith of justification (5).

Other confessions specify the service of the Word, the sacraments and often discipline as marks by which the Church is known or discerned. According to the Genevan Confession, one of the earliest fruits of John Calvin's activity in the city in 1536, 'the proper mark by which rightly to discern the Church of Jesus Christ is that his holy gospel be purely and faithfully preached, proclaimed, heard and kept, and that his sacraments be properly administered' (18). The First Helvetic (Swiss) Confession of the same year, which was the first joint confession of the reformed cities of Switzerland (not yet including Geneva), puts the matter less personally: 'the fellowship and congregation of all saints which is Christ's bride and spouse' is 'not only known but also gathered and built up by visible signs, rites and ordinances, which Christ himself has instituted and appointed by the Word of God as a universal, public and orderly discipline' (14). A simpler statement is given in the Second Helvetic Confession of 1566, which is perhaps the most mature and most widely accepted, as well as the longest, confession of Reformed Protestantism. 'The true Church is that in which the signs or marks of the true Church are to be found, especially the lawful and sincere preaching of the Word of God as it was delivered to us in the books of the prophets and the apostles' (17). This Confession's expansive exposition proceeds to itemise other 'notes or signs of the true Church', including spiritual unity and worship and participation in the sacraments instituted by Christ. No clearer declaration could be asked for than is given in the Scots Confession: 'The notes of the true Kirk we believe, confess and avow to be: first, the true preaching of the Word of God, in which God has revealed himself to us...; secondly, the right administration of the sacraments of Jesus Christ...; and lastly, ecclesiastical discipline uprightly ministered, as God's Word prescribes' (18).

Functional Ministry

It is noteworthy that the confessions we have quoted identify the Church by the activities it engages in, the functions or services that are fulfilled in it, by it and for it, rather than by its possession of certain special individuals (ordained ministers) to carry them out. This is an essentially ecclesial approach to ministry; the preaching of the Word of God and the administration of sacraments and discipline are responsibilities and privileges *of the Church*, before they are entrusted to particular members of the Church. The Church cannot live without the Word and the sacraments, but it may be able to live without officers of a certain kind to dispense them. Such a perspective, which places the ordering of the Church's ministry at one remove from the indispensability of maintaining the Word and the sacraments in the Church, is of immense practical import, not least in the contemporary situation of the Church of Scotland faced by the problems addressed by 'Union and Readjustment' of congregations. The sole *sine qua non* is the provision of the service of Word and sacraments, not the availability of, say, presbyters with official minimum credentials to supply it.

Luther's *Large Catechism* of 1529, which enjoys confessional status in Lutheranism by virtue of its inclusion in the *Book of Concord* (1580), speaks of the Church itself as the ministering agent. In its explanation of the third article of the Apostles Creed ('I believe in the Holy Spirit, the holy Christian Church...'), Luther describes the Church as 'the mother that begets and bears every Christian through the Word of God... There is on earth a little holy flock or community of pure saints under one head, Christ... I was brought to it by the Holy Spirit and incorporated into it through the fact that I have heard and still hear God's Word... Until the last day the Holy Spirit remains with the holy community or Christian people. Through it he gathers us, using it to teach and preach the Word.' Such an emphasis is entirely proper, since the Creed makes no mention of ministers.

The Church Hearing the Word

The confessions give central place to the Church's proclamation of the Word, but they also speak frequently of the Church's obedient hearing of the Word. In this connexion the teaching of Jesus about following the voice of the shepherd (John 10:2-5) is often cited or alluded to. The Ten Theses (Conclusions) of Berne, which were affirmed after a disputation there in 1528 involving a wide range of Reformers from Switzerland and South Germany, begin by affirming that 'The holy Christian Church, whose only head is Christ, is born of the Word of God, abides in the same, and does not listen to the voice of a stranger'. The Genevan Confession insists that the first identifying mark of the Church of Jesus Christ is that 'his holy gospel be purely and faithfully preached, proclaimed, heard and kept... Where the gospel is not declared, heard and received, there we do not acknowledge the form of the Church' (18). According to the Gallican Confession the true Church is 'the company of the faithful who agree to follow God's Word and the pure religion which it teaches... Properly speaking, there can be no Church where the Word of God is not received, nor profession made of subjection to it, nor use of the sacraments' (27, 28). In the Second Helvetic Confession, the stipulation of the lawful and sincere preaching of the Word of God as the primary mark of the Church is followed by a quotation of John 10: 27, 28, 5. Those who 'do not proclaim the voice of the Shepherd undoubtedly cannot represent the Church, the bride of Christ. Therefore they are not to be heard in his name, since Christ's sheep follow not the voice of a stranger' (Tetrapolitan Confession 15). The Westminster Confession correlates the purity of the Church to the gospel being 'taught and embraced' (25:4).

The Church is accordingly to be discerned not merely where the Word is faithfully expounded but where it is received, believed, heeded. This emphasis joins up with the primary definition of the Church in the confessions — 'the assembly of all believers' (Augsburg Confession 7), 'the assembly of true Christian believers' (Belgic Confession 27), 'one company and multitude of men chosen by God who rightly worship and embrace him by true faith in Christ Jesus' (Scots Confession 16). That is to say, the ministry of the Word and sacraments enables the Church to be and become the Church, not by virtue of its due performance alone but by its fruitfulness through the Spirit. It is not preaching and sacraments that *ex opere operato* turn a body of people into the Church, but rather their power in the hands of God to evoke repentance, faith and worship. The Word believed is as essential to the Church as the Word proclaimed.

This is an emphasis that has tended to be obscured in expositions of Reformation doctrines of ministry, which have too often given the impression that the Church is constituted by the ministry of the Word almost regardless of congregational response or even presence. This may have been more of a danger on the Lutheran side, with its more one-sided stress on the objective givenness of the Word of Christ, independent of the response of faith. This is seen in the Reformation debates about the presence of Christ in the Lord's Supper, which Luther refused to make conditional on believing reception, whereas the Zwinglian and Reformed, in different ways, argued that Christ is eaten only by faith. So Lutheran confessional statements typically

DAVID F. WRIGHT

highlight the Spirit's gift of faith through the ministry of the Word
rather than the congregation's heeding the voice of the Shepherd.
Luther's *Large Catechism*, in explaining the sabbath Commandment,
says that 'At whatever time God's Word is taught, preached, heard,
read or pondered, there the person, the day and the work are
sanctified by it'.

The introduction of the Reformation, particularly in the cities of
Switzerland and South Germany, was often effected through a
declaration of assent to the gospel by the people at large, whether in
the citizen assembly, as at Geneva, or in the broadest representative
body, as at Strasbourg, or in disputations. These were somewhat like
large public Bible studies in which the citizens adjudicated whether the
old clergy or the new preachers had more faithfully interpreted the
Scriptures. Such exercises presupposed two fundamental Protestant
convictions, the priesthood of all Christians and the perspicuity of
Scripture. We may discern some echo of this common feature of the
Reformation in these cities in the place the confessions give to the
recognition and following of the voice of the Shepherd as an
indispensable mark of the true Church of Christ.

To make this point may provoke some hard questions. What about
the ministry of the Word in a congregation which extends no
welcoming embrace of faith for years on end? Is there not a proper
comfort to be gained in such a situation from appealing to the
Reformers' primary emphasis on the proclamation of the Word? Is not
the faithfulness of such a ministry rather than its success the decisive
criterion? Perhaps too easy a resort to such considerations should be
viewed as a temptation, as also should taking refuge in the inscrutable
working of divine providence. Is it an unthinkable conclusion that,
where the service of Word and sacraments evokes no response from a
community, such a ministry cannot be viewed as giving that body of
people the dignity of 'the Church'? This must be seen as a reasonable
interpretation of some of the confessional declarations cited above. At
the same time, such a dreadful possibility must assume that it is indeed
the Word of God that is held forth for the hearing of faith. God forbid
that we shake off the dust of our feet because a house or a town has
refused to hear not God's Word but a merely human message. On the
other hand, if the confessions are correct in suggesting that believing
response to the gospel is integral to the proclamation of the Word as a
mark of the Church, those charged with this ministry should be
appropriately confident and expectant. Church growth, in this sense, is
a normal accompaniment of a ministry of gospel Word and
sacraments.

Call and Election

It would be misleading to give the impression that the Reformation
confessions are not interested in the ordering of the ministry. The
Tetrapolitan Confession's chapter on the Office, Dignity and Power of

44

Ministers in the Church precedes that on the Church itself. (Too much, however, should not be made of the sequence of material. Even earlier come chapters on Fasts, Meats and Monkery! Theology is not done by ordinal numbers.) Normally a section is devoted to the Church before any attempt to specify how, or by whom, the ministry of Word, sacraments and discipline is to be exercised. Moreover, the confessions are in the main much more concerned about what ministers should do than about the offices they should occupy or the titles they should bear. There is little warrant in the confessions for making a particular polity mandatory. Several of them, however, do insist that all ministers must enjoy parity of authority. If order is a term which in this area of discussion normally implies hierarchy, then these confessions (with the exception of the Thirty-Nine Articles) know only one order of ministry.

Furthermore, the confessions are far more interested in the congregational call and choice of ministers than in their ordination. The Scots Confession nowhere alludes to the need for ordination; it merely states that the sacraments must be 'ministered by lawful ministers,...men appointed to preach the Word, unto whom God has given the power to preach the gospel, and who are lawfully called by some Kirk.' (The First Book of Discipline confirms that this lack of reference to ordination is no accidental oversight.) Even the Thirty-Nine Articles say only that no-one is to take up the office of 'Ministering in the Congregation' (itself a significant heading) 'before he be lawfully called and sent to execute the same...by men who have public authority given unto them in the congregation, to call and send ministers into the Lord's vineyard' (23). A later article refers to the Ordinal of Edward VI for the arrangements for the ordering of ministers. The Confession of Faith used by the English congregation at Geneva and incorporated into Knox's *Form of Prayers* (1556) merely states that the sacraments are to be administered as Christ has ordained and 'by such as by ordinary vocation are thereunto called' (4).

The Augsburg Confession's one-sentence article on Order in the Church asserts no more than that 'nobody should publicly teach or preach or administer the sacraments in the Church without a regular call' (14). The Catholic *Confutation* of this article demanded the employment of canonical ordination. Melanchthon's *Apology* for the Confession, which was placed alongside it in the *Book of Concord*, partly defers to this demand, professing a commitment to maintain 'the Church polity and various ranks of the ecclesiastical hierarchy, although they were created by human authority', but also affirming that the preservation of canonical order is secondary to advancing the teaching of the Word. A similar note is sounded in two other documents of confessional standing in the *Book of Concord*, Luther's Schmalkald Articles, drawn up for the papal council originally called for Mantua in 1537 which eventually met later at Trent, and

Melanchthon's *Treatise on the Power and Primacy of the Pope* (1537), which was adopted as a supplement to the Augsburg Confession. Both give priority to maintaining the gospel in the Church over the observance of canonical proprieties. As Melanchthon put it, 'Wherever the Church exists, the right to administer the gospel also exists. Wherefore it is necessary for the Church to retain the right of calling, electing and ordaining ministers.'

The Tetrapolitan Confession, which is a counterpart to Augsburg, mediating between Lutherans and Zwinglians, omits all reference to human appointment in its chapter on the Office, Dignity and Power of Ministers in the Church, deeming it sufficient to affirm that 'what constitutes fit and properly consecrated ministers of the Church, bishops, teachers and pastors, is that they have been divinely sent..., i.e., that they have received the power and mind to preach the gospel and feed the flock of Christ' (13). More typical is the Gallican Confession, which holds that the authority of pastors 'should be derived from election, as far as it is possible'. It must at least be a binding rule 'that all pastors, overseers and deacons should have evidence of being called to their office' (31). The Belgic Confession, which largely parallels the Gallican, similarly, if more allusively, stipulates 'a lawful election of the Church, with calling upon the name of the Lord, and in that order which the Word of God teaches' (31). More explicit is the First Helvetic Confession, although the emphasis remains the same. The 'administrative power...to preach God's Word and to tend the flock of the Lord' is to be conferred only on those qualified by divine calling and election and by the Church's approval (16). They must be 'recognized and accepted by the judgment of the Church and the laying on of hands by the elders' (17). What is required according to the Second Helvetic Confession are careful calling and election 'by the Church or by those delegated from the Church for that purpose', followed by ordination with public prayer and laying on of hands (18).

Thus the confessions are more concerned with the bond between minister and congregation than between minister and any ministerial *ordo*, class or court. The significant lines of connexion are with the congregation, not with a body of ministers extended in time (by succession) or space (in presbyteries or similar institutions). In so far as the confessions are interested in historical continuity, it is the continuity of the Church, not the 'lineal succession' (Scots Confession 18) of ministers. The Reformation rejected 'absolute' ordination, i.e., ordination without reference to a specific charge. The ministry made sense only in relation to a local congregation, and so ordination was much less important than the congregational call. Ordination was little more than confirmation within the congregation of its calling and election of a person, not initiation into a supra-congregational order of ministers.

Outward and Inward Teaching

Lutheran confessional statements elevated the external ministry of Word and sacraments in opposition to the prominence given to the inner enlightenment and experience of the Spirit by Radical Protestants. 'Condemned are the Anabaptists and others who teach that the Holy Spirit comes to us through our own preparations, thoughts and works without the external Word of the gospel' (Augsburg Confession 5). The sharpest Lutheran statement to this effect comes in the Schmalkald Articles. 'God gives no one his Spirit or grace except through or with the external Word which comes before...God will not deal with us except through his external Word or sacrament. Whatever is attributed to the Spirit apart from such Word and sacrament is of the devil' (8). Only occasionally is the point made so bluntly in the Reformed confessions, although their uniform stress on the indispensability of the proclamation by Word and sacrament undoubtedly owes something to the desire to dissociate themselves from the Radicals' spiritualism. This is especially clear in confessions that are apologetically motivated. Thus the Gallican Confession maintains that 'the Church cannot exist without pastors for instruction'. Although God is not bound to such means, nevertheless the Confession rejects all visionaries who would destroy the ministry of Word and sacraments (25).

More space in the Reformed confessions is devoted to the relationship between human agency and the working of God. It goes without saying that all of them regard the ministry of the gospel as the means by which not only is the true Church distinguishable from the false, but the Church is itself created and built up by God. Several evince a concern that the distinctive roles of God and man should not be confused. The Tetrapolitan Confession quotes 1 Corinthians 3:6 ('I planted, Apollos watered, but God gave the growth') to show that no persons should be thought of as more than ministers of Christ and stewards of the mysteries of God. They have the keys of the kingdom, but 'in such a manner that they are nothing else than ministers of Christ, whose right and prerogative alone this is' (13). 'The Church's ministers are God's co-workers..., through whom he imparts and offers to those who believe in him the knowledge of himself and the forgiveness of sins,... but in all things we ascribe all efficacy and power to God the Lord alone, and only the imparting to the minister' (First Helvetic Confession 15). The sacraments are 'signs of divine grace by which the ministers of the Church work with the Lord...Bread and wine are...signs by which the true communion of his body and blood is administered and offered to believers by the Lord himself by means of the ministry of the Church' (20, 22).

As on many issues, the Second Helvetic Confession gives an extended and balanced account. Outward preaching is not rendered pointless by the need for inward illumination. The Lord inwardly opened Lydia's heart as Paul preached to her. Although God can illumine whom and when he will, even without the external ministry, it is not his usual way (1). In the New Testament the apostolic preaching is called 'the Spirit' and 'the ministry of the Spirit' because 'by faith it becomes effectual and living in the ears, nay more, in the hearts of believers through the illumination of the Holy Spirit' (13). We must neither 'attribute what has to do with our conversion and instruction to the secret power of the Holy Spirit in such a way that we make void the ecclesiastical ministry', nor 'ascribe too much to ministers and the ministry'. God teaches both outwardly and inwardly at the same time (18). Christ reserves his authority to himself and does not transfer it to any other, 'so that he might stand idly by as a spectator while his ministers work'. Yet when they do what their Lord commands, *they* may be said to open the kingdom to the obedient and shut it to the disobedient. Their ministry is such that 'they reconcile men to God..., remit sins..., and rightly and effectually absolve when they preach the gospel of Christ' (14).

Such a conjunction between the work of the Spirit and human ministry suggests how congregations should honour the latter. 'As we receive the true ministers of the Word of God as messengers and ambassadors of God, it is necessary to listen to them as to God himself' (Genevan Confession 20). The first chapter of the Second Helvetic Confession deals with Scripture as the true Word of God. In testimony thereto it cites 1 Thessalonians 2:13, Matthew 10:20, Luke 10:16 and John 13:20. 'When this Word of God is now preached in the Church by preachers lawfully called, we believe that the very Word of God is proclaimed, and received by the faithful.' As the sub-heading puts it, in a memorable phrase, 'The preaching of the Word of God is the Word of God'.

Limitations

The weaknesses of the confessions lie close to their strengths. They display little awareness that others in the congregation beside preachers, pastors, elders and deacons may have ministries to fulfil. Statements such as 'the Church acknowledges no ministry except that which preaches the Word of God and administers the sacrament' (Lausanne Articles 5, 1536) must not be interpreted outside their polemical context. Nevertheless, very rare is the note sounded by the Tetrapolitan Confession: 'Since it is the Church and kingdom of God, and for this reason all things must be done in the best order, it has various offices of ministers. For it is a body compacted of various members, whereof each has his own work' (15). In his *Large Catechism* Luther explains that the community of Christians is 'called together by the Holy Spirit in one faith, mind and understanding. It possesses a variety of gifts, yet it is united in love without sect or schism. Of this community I also am a part and a member, a participant and co-partner in all the blessings it possesses.' Yet there is little development towards an organic concept of the Church and the mutual responsibilities of all its members.

Not one of the confessions even inculcates the responsibility of the faithful to pray for ministers. Luther's *Small Catechism*, likewise part of the *Book of Concord*, includes a Table of Duties spelt out in lists of biblical verses. The Duties Christians Owe Their Teachers and Pastors are to be found in Luke 10:7, 1 Corinthians 9:14, Galatians 6:6-7, 1 Timothy 5:17-18 (which all deal with 'the maintenance of the ministry'), 1 Thessalonians 5:12-13 (respect and esteem), and Hebrews 13:17 (submission). The limitations of such a list are only too obvious.

The paramount duty of Christian people is that of diligent attendance at worship for the hearing of the Word. This is regularly emphasised as the import of the sabbath Commandment, which teaches that 'we should not despise God's Word and the preaching of it, but deem it holy and gladly hear and learn it' (Luther's *Small Catechism*). The Gallican Confession allows no absence, even in persecution: 'We believe that no-one ought to seclude himself and be contented to be alone; but that all jointly should keep and maintain the union of the Church, and submit to the public teaching, and to the yoke of Jesus Christ, wherever God shall have established a true order of the Church, even if the magistrates and their edicts are contrary to it' (26).

The ultimate justification for such insistence was that the gifts of life, righteousness and the Holy Spirit 'cannot be obtained except through the office of preaching and of administering the holy sacraments', as the Augsburg Confession expressed it (28). Almost half a century later, the Formula of Concord (1577) settled decades of doctrinal dispute among Lutherans. The issues in contention included the role of free will in conversion and regeneration. The Formula's Solid Declaration on this question contained the following section on 'how and by what means (namely, the oral Word and the holy sacraments) the Holy Spirit wills to be efficacious in us by giving and working true repentance, faith and new spiritual power and ability for good in our hearts, and how we are to relate ourselves to and use these means:

> In his boundless kindness and mercy, God provides for the public proclamation of his divine, eternal law and the wonderful counsel concerning our redemption, namely, the holy and only saving gospel of his eternal Son, our only Saviour and Redeemer, Jesus Christ. Thereby he gathers an eternal church for himself out of the human race and works in the hearts of men true repentance and knowledge of their sins and true faith in the Son of God, Jesus Christ. And it is God's will to call men to eternal salvation, to draw them to himself, convert them, beget them anew, and sanctify them through this means and in no other way — namely, through his holy Word (when one hears it preached or reads it) and the sacraments (when they are used according to his Word) (1 Cor. 1:21; Acts 11:14; Rom. 10:17; John 17:17, 20; Matt. 17:5). All who would be saved must hear this preaching, for the preaching and the hearing of God's Word are the Holy Spirit's instrument in, with, and through which he wills to act efficaciously, to convert men to God, and to work in them both to will and to achieve.

The person who is not yet converted to God and regenerated can hear and read this Word externally because, as stated above, even after the Fall man still has something of a free will in these external matters, so that he can go to church, listen to the sermon, or not listen to it.

Through this means (namely, the preaching and the hearing of his Word) God is active, breaks our hearts, and draws man, so that through the preaching of the law man learns to know his sins and the wrath of God and experiences genuine terror, contrition, and sorrow in his heart, and through the preaching of and meditation upon the holy gospel of the gracious forgiveness of sins in Christ there is kindled in him a spark of faith which accepts the forgiveness of sins for Christ's sake and comforts itself with the promise of the gospel. And in this way the Holy Spirit, who works all of this, is introduced into the heart.

On the one hand, it is true that both the preacher's planting and watering and the hearer's running and willing would be in vain, and no conversion would follow, if there were not added the power and operation of the Holy Spirit, who through the Word preached and heard illuminates and converts hearts so that men believe this Word and give their assent to it. On the other hand, neither the preacher nor the hearer should question this grace and operation of the Holy Spirit, but should be certain that, when the Word of God is preached, pure and unalloyed according to God's command and will, and when the people diligently and earnestly listen to and meditate on it, God is certainly present with his grace and gives what man is unable by his own powers to take or to give. We should not and cannot pass judgment on the Holy Spirit's presence, operations, and gifts merely on the basis of our feeling, how and when we perceive it in our hearts. On the contrary, because the Holy Spirit's activity often is hidden, and happens under cover of great weakness, we should be certain, because of and on the basis of his promise, that the Word which is heard and preached is an office and work of the Holy Spirit, whereby he assuredly is potent and active in our hearts (2 Cor. 2:14ff.).

For living proof of the truth of this fine statement, one could do no better than observe what God has wrought through the preaching of William Still, *minister Verbi Dei*, whom we salute on this notable anniversary.

CHURCH AND MINISTRY IN 1 TIMOTHY

I. HOWARD MARSHALL

It has been observed by no less a scholar than Rudolf Bultmann that presuppositionless exegesis is impossible; that is to say, we cannot avoid being influenced in our study of Scripture by all that has gone to make us what we are, and therefore we must at least try to be aware of our predispositions and allow for them in our study. I first sat in Gilcomston South Church of Scotland in 1946 shortly after William Still began his ministry there, and before long I became a fairly regular attender at Sunday evening services and mid-week Bible Studies. A continuing personal friendship with Willie, developed especially during my period of leadership of the Evangelical Union in the University, and the impact of his preaching and teaching during my student years have been a major influence in my life. Whether, therefore, what follows in this essay represents 'objective' study of the New Testament or whether it has been influenced by what I have learned from William Still is left to the reader to judge; for my part I believe that this important 'presupposition' in my life has led me to perceive more clearly what is objectively there in the New Testament, and for this I am grateful to God and to his servant as a minister of his Word.

The question of ministry in 1 Timothy and in the Pastorals generally is probably the most discussed topic in these letters. Many people would trace, rightly or wrongly, a kind of evolution of church order from the rudiments that we find in Paul's earliest epistles (1 Thess. and Gal.) to the more developed charismatic type of situation reflected in 1 Corinthians and then on to the more settled and regulated type of system in the Pastorals. This evolution can then be traced in the direction of a more elaborate and rigid system in the developing catholic church, and it has probably affected most of mainstream Christianity in our day. Nevertheless, there has been a return to a type of charismatic church order in certain quarters today, and of course there has always been a tradition of a much more free type of church order in so-called Free Church circles. Since the Pastorals contain some of the fullest teaching on ministry, it is not surprising that people regularly turn to them for guidance on this topic. In view of the reconsideration of charismatic influences in the church today the question of what the Pastorals teach is all the more interesting. We shall confine our attention to 1 Timothy, and it will be helpful for us first of all to consider the nature of the church as seen in the epistle.

The Nature of the Church

The word church (*ekklesia*) is found only three times in 1 Timothy.

We can pass over 5:16 where the word 'church' simply refers to the local congregation. The other two uses are more significant. In 3:5 the qualifications for a bishop include that he must be able to manage his household well, since otherwise he will not be able to care for God's church. This suggests that there is some similarity between the church and a household, and this is confirmed by the remaining text, 3:15, which refers to 'the household of God, which is the church of the living God, the pillar and bulwark of the truth'. The word translated 'household' is simply *oikos* which can mean a house as a building but here must mean the entire set-up of a family including husband, wife, children and any other relatives together with the slaves. The church functions in the same sort of way as a family of this kind. The picture of the church as a house also appears in 2 Tim. 2:20f. which refers to the various utensils that may be used by the master of the house.

The term 'house' has a history in relation to its use with reference to God. A house is usually thought of as a dwelling, and it was common for a temple to be known as the house of God; this phrase is used of the Jewish temple or its predecessor, the tabernacle, in Mk. 2:26; 11:17; Jn. 2:16f. In the OT the idea that the temple is the actual house of God, as in some pagan religions, is avoided. The temple is rather the place where God is present to communicate with his people, and it is recognised that he is too great to be confined within a manmade building. In the NT it is recognised that God is present in the midst of his believing people. It is they rather than a building who constitute the temple or shrine of God, and this can be affirmed by Paul both of the individual believer (1 Cor. 6:19) whose body is the temple *(naos)* of the Holy Spirit and also of the community of believers who form the temple of God in which the Holy Spirit dwells and who are therefore holy (1 Cor. 3:16f.). It is interesting that in this context Paul thinks of the church as a building erected upon a foundation which is Christ himself; here Paul is thinking of the local congregation at Corinth, and when he says that he himself laid the foundation it seems probable that he is thinking of the apostolic teaching about Jesus. We find that Paul also speaks of believers as forming the temple of God in 2 Cor. 6:16 and therefore as people who cannot consistently join themselves to the worshippers of idols; God is in their midst and therefore they are his holy people. Further, we have the important passage in Ephesians 2:19-22 where believers, both Jews and Gentiles, form the house or household of God, built upon a solid foundation of the apostles and prophets (which must surely be a reference to their teaching) and with Christ as the principal stone; thus they form a holy temple in which God dwells by the Spirit. Here, then, we have the thoughts of the family or household and the temple closely joined together.

In 1 Tim. 3:15 the idea of the household is probably the dominant one. Is it significant that the writer talks about the house of God and then goes on to explain that it is the church rather than talking about the church and then going on to explain that it is the household of God?

Why this strange form of expression? It seems that his uppermost thought is that of the conduct which is appropriate for those who are members or leaders in the household of God, and which has already come to expression in 3:5. Then he goes on to qualify the household of God by stating two further things about it.

The first is that it is the church *of the living God*. What is the fresh point that is being made by this addition which seems rather superfluous? It may be significant that already in 2 Cor. 6:16 Paul has spoken of believers as constituting a temple and he states that it is the temple of the living God. The reference to the house of God as being the church of the *living* God may well suggest that the thought is partly of the living presence of God among his people. The intention may be to emphasise the solemnity of the instructions. Thus the idea of a discipline within the church comes to expression. And this may be important in view of the presence of heresy within the church. Heresy is inconsistent with obedience to the Lord. Furthermore, may there be a hint that the church is indeed *the ekklesia* of God? It is *the* people of God over against the Jewish synagogue, and therefore the attempt of the heretics to turn it into a synagogue is uncalled for.

The fact that heresy is in mind is further to be seen in the second qualification, namely that the church is *the pillar and foundation of the truth*. The expression tends to identify the truth with the church rather than to say that the church is merely a sort of outside buttress which helps to prop up a truth which somehow exists independently of it. The church is to be the place where the truth is found, and thus it must be the entity by which the truth is supported. The truth is almost thought of as a sort of roof held up by a pillar established on a solid foundation. Yet at the same time the church is surely itself based on the truth. Hence the importance of truth in the church is stressed, and once again the background of heresy in the church comes to mind. The church must stand firm as the defender of the truth against heresy.

Thus the maintenance of godly order in the church, which depends upon a properly instituted set of leaders, is closely tied up with the character of the church as the foundation of truth. It is because of the nature of the church as the foundation of the truth over against the attacks of heresy that there must be such care taken about the character of its leaders. All this leads naturally to the question of the function of the leaders.

The Importance of Teaching

One of the points that most demands attention in the present-day church is the great emphasis in the NT generally and especially in 1 Timothy on teaching as a central activity in early Christian meetings. Our tendency is to think of such meetings as being for the primary purpose of worship, in the sense of the service that we render to God. Consequently the attention gets directed to liturgy, which of course means service, and to what we do towards God. For some people the word 'liturgical' seems to mean rather the involvement of the members of the congregation in some kind of verbal and even bodily activity by the provision of responses and other material in which everybody can join, instead of just sitting passively except for rising to sing hymns and putting one's hand into the collection plate. Insofar as 'liturgical' signifies the involvement of the congregation I am all for it. But the word can shift the emphasis away from something else that is vital. It is the fact that the church meeting is a place for our listening to what God has to say to us. Two activities take place simultaneously. The one is that we all of us listen to what the Lord our God has to say to us. We come together to hear his word. The other thing is that his word must be declared, and this is done by some of the very people who are there to listen to it. They share their listening with others and so become the agents of God's further speaking to the congregation as a whole.

The problem which surfaces in 1 Timothy is the activity of people who are promoting strange ideas in the church that are not in accord with the author's understanding of the Christian faith and in fact take people away from it. Heresy can of course have disastrous effects on behaviour, but the starting point is usually in false teaching. And it is this that is a major concern in 1 Timothy. The author sees a twofold antidote to it.

On the one hand, he stresses the importance of Christian character, especially faith and love, and he wants to divert attention from heretical teaching that leads to dissension and to turn his congregations to genuine love and harmony. But at the same time he sees the need to engage with heresy by presenting sound teaching in its place. He will not waste time in futile arguments over nonsense, but at the same time he is prepared to discuss with people in the church who are misled and some parts of the letter are meant to be a reply to heretical teaching (1:8-11; 4:4f.; 6:6-10). But above all he wants to see the true faith properly presented. He doesn't use the Pauline word 'edification' *(oikodome)*, but that is what he has in mind.

This points us to one of the great stresses of the letters. The writer sees the main duty of all Christian 'leaders' (we use this vague word for the moment) as being teaching. A study of the vocabulary used in the letter would quickly establish how important this theme is. But the most helpful way for us to approach the matter may be to look quickly at the various church leaders who are mentioned.

(1) What is the picture of *Paul himself?* The whole letter consists of instructions to be taught to the congregation which he is transmitting to Timothy to pass on to them. He presents himself as a preacher and apostle and a teacher (2:7). The verse is intriguing. The use of preacher, Gk. *keryx,* herald, is found only here and in 2 Tim. 1:11 where the same triad is repeated, and in 2 Pet. 2:5 of Noah (who may be tacitly a 'type' for the Christian preacher). 'Apostle' we already know as Paul's favourite self-description, but here the company it

keeps must give it a particular sense. 'Teacher' is the operative word, linked as it is to 'of the Gentiles'; Paul does not use it of himself in his earlier letters. Now is this picture of Paul as teacher 'different' and hence possibly emphatic? It is certainly in harmony with his earlier picture of himself. Paul regards himself as the instructor of his congregations, who gives them commands and exhortations to follow. Similarly in Acts 11:26 the function of Paul along with Barnabas at Antioch is to teach the church. The picture seems to me to be a consistent one. The fact that Paul is an apostle gives his teaching authority. This is apparent from the way in which in 2 Tim. 1:13 Paul speaks of the pattern of sound words which Timothy has received from him. See also 2 Tim. 2:2; 3:14. Thus when Paul is described here as a teacher, this simply brings out the meaning of the word 'apostle'; earlier in 1 Cor. 4:1 he described himself and Apollos as 'servants of Christ and stewards of the mysteries of God', and the point here is just the same.

(2) Next we should look at the situation of *Timothy*. The word which sums up his position is 'servant (Gk. *diakonos*) of Jesus Christ' (4:6) which indicates formally at least his position. But this is straightway expanded by reference to his being nourished on the words of the faith and of the good doctrine which he has followed. Timothy is thus able to be a servant of Jesus Christ inasmuch as he has been taught. His duties, therefore, are public reading, preaching and teaching. The first of these is generally understood to be the reading of the OT, but it is possible that by this date the reading of early Christian documents was in mind. We may find a hint in this direction in 5:18 where the writer quotes both an Old Testament text (Dt. 25:4) and a saying of Jesus recorded in Lk. 10:7 as being from 'the scripture'. Again Timothy is to take heed to his teaching, so that he may save both himself and his hearers. Thus his role as a teacher is clear.

(3) As for the *church leaders* who are to be appointed, we note that there are some elders who labour in preaching and teaching and are to be given double honour. The qualifications for the potential bishop include, admittedly rather incidentally, that he is to be apt to teach (3:3; cf. Tit. 1:9). His other tasks involve caring for the church, and that is all that is said; from the lack of mention of other duties we may safely argue that teaching was an essential element in his task. It should be observed that the noun translated 'preaching' (Gk. *logos)* is really to be translated 'word'. 'Word' and 'teaching' are joined together in 6:3 and 'word' and 'doctrine' in 4:6; hence we can assume that the activity of the elders is primarily in doctrinal teaching.

(4) Were there *any other teachers* in the church? We hear of prophetic utterances in connection with the 'ordination' of Timothy (1:18; 4:14), and also there are reports of prophetic utterances by the Spirit regarding conditions in the last days (4:1), but nothing is said about who exercised this ministry. We certainly cannot rule out the existence of persons with the gift of prophecy as in 1 Cor. 12 and

elsewhere.

(5) Is it significant that some of the 'heretics' wanted to be *'teachers of the law'?* Where exactly does this fit into the life of the church? I suspect that these people may have wished to turn the church back into a kind of synagogue. If so, this would further confirm that the church was seen as a place for teaching, since this is precisely what the synagogue itself was.

From all this it emerges that a major element in the life of the church was teaching, and that the need arose particularly from the fact that the heresy was being promulgated by people who were acting as teachers. They probably wanted to turn the church back into some kind of synagogue with 'teachers of the law' as its leading members. The author holds that bad teaching is to be dealt with by better teaching, by the clear and compelling presentation of the apostolic tradition.

Church Leaders

We have singled out the importance of teaching in 1 Timothy as one of the elements which arises out of the nature of the church, namely in its function as the foundation and pillar of the truth. Now we take a further look at the task of leadership or management which arises out of the nature of the church as the household of God.

In 3:1 the writer speaks about the character of a bishop. By this term we are to understand a local church leader, probably also known as an elder in view of the clear equation in Tit. 1:5, 7. It is often thought that elders and bishops are synonymous terms, so that there would have been a plurality of bishops in a local church, but it is possible that by this time a smaller number of people, or even only one, within a local group of elders were being given special tasks as bishops. The task of a bishop is said to be a good work. Elsewhere good works are spoken of in a broad sense (5:10, 25; 6:18) and they are to be the characteristic of all believers. But a narrower sense seems demanded here in the context. The writer appears rather to be commending the desire to act as a church leader of this kind.

The writer is mainly concerned with the character of the potential bishop. He has to fulfil various requirements, which can be summarised as:

(1) Living at a standard of morality recognised by secular society at large, and hence having a good reputation among people outside the church. This point can be demonstrated by observing how some of the qualities are the same as those found in secular lists of the time setting out the qualities required for various kinds of officials.

(2) Having a character that is the opposite of that which the writer ascribes to the heretics. If we were to compare the vices of the heretics who are condemned in the Pastoral Epistles with the good qualities desired in church leaders, we should find that there are many correspondences between them. This indicates that part of the reason for the appointment of bishops is to deal with the heretical situation in the church.

(3) Having various characteristics directly related to his role in the church. A bishop must be hospitable: this may refer both to welcoming travelling Christians and to welcoming the church into his home. (This is a characteristic of believers in general in 1 Pet. 4:9). He must be able to teach. He must be able to manage his own household well and this means that he must be able to command obedience from his children. Otherwise he will not be able to lead the church, since the church is thought of as a household. We thus have in effect three church-related characteristics: hospitality; teaching ability; firm leadership.

Thus there were people in the church who had some kind of authority over the other members. The extreme case of the exercise of such authority would be in the excommunication of members, exercised by Paul himself in the case of Hymenaeus and Alexander (1:20) and earlier by the church meeting at Corinth (1 Cor. 5). But we are told very little about how the bishops were to lead the church, and our best policy may be to consider the role ascribed to Timothy himself and assume that the task of a bishop would be modelled on his.

Since the deacons are discussed after the bishops, and since the description is shorter, it seems likely that they are less important. The actual word 'deacon' (Gk. *diakonos)* is of course used for all servants in the church. The qualifications are similar to those for bishops. There is no mention of their leading the church, but they are not to be greedy for gain, which may suggest financial responsibilities in charitable care. But they are also to hold the mystery of the faith with a good conscience, which might perhaps suggest a teaching role. They are also not to serve unless they have fulfilled a period of probation; this is probably to avoid the possibility that they are recent converts (as in 3:6). It is not clear whether bishops were to be chosen from among the deacons. Only men with wives and households are in mind. If they do their job well (cf. 5:17) they gain a good 'stand' for themselves and much assurance in the faith. Again the wording is obscure. It is unlikely to mean a step in promotion and is more likely to be a 'good standing' or reputation; one commentator appears to suggest that they have a good position from which to evangelise and also that they gain in assurance, which may mean the ability to witness in the world. Unfortunately deacons are not mentioned again in the Pastorals, so we are left in the dark about their functions. Space prevents a discussion of whether 3:11 refers to deacons' wives or to female deacons.

Next we must ask about the elders who are mentioned in 5:17 and how they are related to the other leaders. Those who lead well — the word is the same as in 3:5 — are to receive double honour. Perhaps this just means additional honour. In any case it distinguishes one group of elders either from those who do not 'lead' at all or from those who do so badly or perhaps from those who have minor as opposed to major responsibilities. Included among those to receive double honour are especially those who labour in word and teaching. This suggests that the reference is to those who have greater functions. Now this takes us back to the reference to elders in 5:1 where Timothy is told not to rebuke older men; the word is the same, but the reference here must be simply to people in the older age group. They are to be respected because of their age. The implication is that Timothy is a young office-bearer. Does the word *presbyteros* then simply mean 'old person' throughout, as has sometimes been urged? There are difficulties with this view (especially in 4:14 which suggests that an office of eldership existed or that the old men/elders ordained Timothy, and in Tit. 1:5 unless this verse means that Titus is to appoint certain of the old men as bishops). Nevertheless, it may give a good sense here. It may well be that there was a certain fluidity in church organisation with the result that the older men generally exercised a role in the community by reason of their age, and some were preeminent among the others by doing the tasks of the bishops. The situation is problematic in that in the ancient world there were only the two categories of young men and old men, with the rather hazy dividing line coming at the age of forty. There was to be respect shown by the young to the old, and this could cause problems with young church leaders like Timothy (4:12) and probably Titus (cf. Tit. 2:15). Travelling missionaries must have included younger people who were fit for the task in a way in which older people were not. Moreover in the local church we also have people who seek to be bishops. Thus in some cases younger people might be specially marked out to be church leaders (what is known in the academic world as 'accelerated promotion'), while in the case of the older people they were at least honoured and had some influence simply through being old people.

As for the position of Timothy himself, he is regarded by Paul as his co-worker and fellow missionary. He is best understood as having the office or function of an evangelist, a person who fulfils a role like Paul himself as a church-planter to use the modern jargon. He is in charge of the churches in the area of Ephesus. Here the analogy of Titus, left in Crete to appoint bishops in every town, is in mind. On this view Timothy functions like Paul himself with authority given him by a group of church leaders (4:14) including Paul himself (2 Tim. 1:6). Although he occupies a supervisory position over a number of churches (perhaps akin to a diocesan bishop in the modern sense), he nevertheless is to demonstrate the kind of character and qualifications that should be shown by church leaders in general. The whole of the Pastoral Epistles thus function as a pattern for all church leaders and ministers.

Conclusion

In our discussion we began from the comments on the nature of the church in 3:14-16 and saw that the church is seen both as the foundation of the truth and as the household of God. The teaching about ministry in the epistle is related to these two characteristics.

(1) On the one hand, great stress is laid on the need for *teaching*

which will expound the apostolic gospel and will enable the church to resist heresy. It goes without saying that the character of the teacher must be in harmony with his message. This emphasis on teaching as what takes place when God's people gather together as a church is fully in line with Paul's emphasis in 1 Cor. 14:26 that the purpose of the various activities in the meeting is to edify or build up the congregation.

Critics have sometimes claimed that the Pastoral Epistles lay too much emphasis on the preservation of the apostolic deposit. The truth handed down from the past is to be handed on, and there is said to be little if any scope for creativity in the formulation of the message. Truth has become 'static' in a manner unlike Paul. This criticism ignores the fact that Christianity is concerned with the handing down of the faith once delivered to the saints; an initial period of great creativity is to be followed by the preservation of the apostolic witness. The emphasis of the Pastorals on this point is a necessary one.

Whenever there is heresy abroad, then the church must respond with a return to fundamentals. There can still be room for a creative approach to Christian doctrine, bearing in mind that 'the Lord hath more light and truth yet to break forth out of His holy word', but the contribution of the Pastorals is to remind us that creativity can go astray and that the tradition must be firmly held to. It may be that those who are most critical of 1 Timothy on this point are themselves not sufficiently appreciative that the faith has been handed down once and for all to God's people.

(2) On the other hand, it is necessary that the household of God be led by people who are qualified to give it proper *direction and oversight*. But what exactly does 'managing' the church as the household of God mean? The fact that church leaders must be able to manage their own households well suggests that *mutatis mutandis* the leaders of the church must have a similar function. The church meetings have to be organised. One must decide where and when they will be held, possibly who will take part in them, to whom charitable relief is to be given, who is to be listed as a widow, what action is to be taken against heretics, whether discipline is to be called for, and so on. These activities require that people take wise decisions on behalf of the community; even if they are decided by discussion among the members (or by whatever method enables the church to hear the Spirit's guidance), there must still be people to carry them out and no doubt in the course of doing so to use their own initiative and commonsense in making further decisions. Such people may have to tell other members of the community what to do, and their instructions are to be accepted and followed. They have to set an example that others will follow by the moral force of their personality and conduct. All this is involved in leadership.

It is interesting that the use of the verb translated 'manage' (Gk. *prohistemi)* is found as early in Paul's writings as 1 Th. 5:12 where it is clear that some kind of leadership is present in the church, even though the church also has charismatic ministry. The same thought is also present in 1 Cor. 16:15f. where the subordination of the church to certain people is demanded, namely to people who are involved as Paul's fellow workers in labouring and in the service of the saints. Thus beside the charismatic roles in the church meeting there is a leadership role by some people, including the first converts.

As far back, then, as we can trace in the Pauline churches, we may observe the presence of leaders who held some kind of more permanent role and alongside them the activity of persons who exercised charismatic gifts. To be sure, 'official' and charismatic roles are not to be equated with leadership and teaching respectively. The various tasks in the church cannot be rigidly separated. 'Management' of the church is charismatic in that some of the gifts of the Spirit in 1 Cor. 12:28 are directly connected with it, and the bishops in 1 Tim. are to be able to teach. Thus the more charismatic pattern in 1 Cor. and the more 'official' pattern here need not be seen as so very far apart. If the stress in 1 Timothy tends to fall on the need for appointed leaders more than on the duty of each member of the congregation to seek for the gifts of the Spirit, this may be due to the exigencies of the situation, where the presence of heresy demanded a more 'fixed' type of leadership, and should not necessarily be taken as the one and only model for all time.

We see that there are tasks of ministry = teaching and ministry = leadership in the church. In both aspects of ministry the crucial function is to guard what has been entrusted to us by the Lord and to act as his servants.

CONCERNING CONFESSIONS

FRANCIS LYALL

I owe much to William Still, both spiritually and otherwise. He has been my minister for now some twenty-eight years, and it is a pleasure to join with the other contributors in this celebration of him. It is a mark of the man and the influence of his ministry that we come from such a variety of backgrounds and disciplines, though naturally there is some bias to the theological in our ranks. Were that bias missing one would have grounds for inquiry.

The topic here mused upon bridges from my own discipline of Law to that of Theology. What follows seeks not to reopen recent discussion, nor any wounds from the years the Kirk has spent on it. I am a lawyer concerned with matters of Public Law, with constitutions and the workings of government and society. That training perhaps affects my perception of such matters. Be that as it may, I am here interested in confessions from a non-theological viewpoint, and I draw on reading of confessions in a variety of jurisdictions. Our experience at Gilcomston South is not, however, irrelevant. It has confirmed for me the importance of confessions, and indeed the importance of the Westminster Confession. But that is to anticipate.

One of the curiosities of modern debates on confessions is how the nature of a church as a human society working within the legal system of a country is usually excluded from consideration. In Scotland it may have something to do with the magnificent statements in the Articles Declaratory of the Constitution of the Church of Scotland in Matters Spiritual in which the Church asserts its independence of the civil authority. Those Articles were, however, adopted as a package, negotiated, over a period of years, between the United Free Church and the Church of Scotland.[1] The Church of Scotland Act 1921, by which the lawfulness of the Articles was enacted by the civil authority, was then passed by Parliament.[2] Only when the legal side of things had been thus secured were the Articles adopted by the Church of Scotland, and the Union of 1929 between that church and the bulk of the United Free Church entered into. In so doing, however, the Church did not slough off its prior history nor its identity. Indeed, its identity, running back to the Reformation, is proudly claimed in the third of the Declaratory Articles.

---

1. R. Sjolinder, *Presbyterian Reunion in Scotland, 1907-1921*, trans. E. J. Sharpe, 1962 Acta Universitatis Upsalensis Studia Historico-Ecclesiastica Upsalensie No. 4.
2. F. Lyall, *Of Presbyters and Kings,* Aberdeen U.P., 1980; F. Lyall, 'The Westminster Confession: The Legal Position', in A. I. C. Heron ed., *The Westminster Confession in the Church Today,* Edinburgh, St Andrew Press, 1982, pp. 55-71. It is understood that a Legal Opinion given by Sir Thomas B. Smith, Q.C., to the Presbytery of Lothian, dated 25th January 1983, agrees substantially with the views as to the powers of the Church of Scotland expressed in the second cited discussion.

The establishment of identity is an important purpose of a Confession. 'Identity' is a curious word. According to the Oxford English Dictionary it appears in the Latin of the fifth century A.D. as a noun of condition or quality, invented to express the notion of 'sameness' and to augment such concepts as 'likeness' and 'oneness'. There are differing views as to its exact development, but the root in the Latin *idem — the same* seems incontrovertible. That root also gives rise to the word 'identification', the perception of identity between apparently separate things.

Even limited interaction between individuals requires some sort of common purpose — 'can two walk together except they be agreed?' (Amos 3:3). Within any grouping a degree of common purpose must be present for any organisation to exist. It is that purpose which must be 'the same' for there to be any coherent activity. It is also often useful that those who are called to direct the organisation shall understand or adhere to the common purpose to a degree not required by the ordinary member. And finally, in relation to outsiders, a display of the purpose held in common allows others to be attracted.

A confession of faith serves such purposes within a church or within a denomination. The beliefs held in common are expressed in the confession. Usually the more technical or 'difficult' elements are required to be acceded to by the elders and ministers, to whom the direction of the church is entrusted. And, as far as the outside world is concerned, the confession serves as a prospectus, indicating the doctrine which is preached within that church. Such at least would seem to be the desirable position.

The history of the church general shows all these elements. Who Jesus was and is, and what he taught, are matters of the utmost importance. If he is the way of salvation there is nothing more important. If he is one among other wise ethical teachers, then there is less urgency in the matter, for others have covered much the same ground, and some have framed their precepts more congenially and with more consideration for the weaknesses of human nature. At that stage, whether one follows Confucius or Christ may be a matter of culture and habit rather than conviction.

The early church was faced with various problems. The truths of the Gospel had to be communicated accurately. Error had to be combatted. What was held in common by the Christians should be stated so that these individuals could know who believed the same things that they did — a matter of practical necessity when, soon, persecution began and questions of security might be involved.

The record starts before the end of the New Testament. First, the purity of the message of Jesus had to be preserved. John speaks of 'many deceivers, who do not acknowledge Jesus Christ as coming in the flesh' (2 John 7). Paul talks of those who teach error, in such passages as 1 Timothy 1:19-20 and 2 Timothy 2:17-18. These adventurers were not conforming to what had been laid out in such statements as 1 Corinthians 15:3-8, where, New Testament scholars tell us, certain of the *thats* indicate quotation.

Again, *bona fides* might have to be established. Paul begins his Letter to the Romans with what amounts to a short poem of faith (Romans 1:1-4). It would make sense for him to start that letter with a statement of their common faiths. After all, the Romans had only *heard* of Paul, and no doubt there were some in that church who were not too sure of him — the Jews would have seen to that.

In these instances Paul may have used his own words. It is, however, also possible, that he may have been reciting a series of propositions in common currency (almost like choruses) at the time. It is likely that, prior to the writing of the books of the New Testament, such simple propositional statements, almost formulae, were the way in which people held on to the basic Christian message which had been preached to them. They did not have our Bible to help them, and yet the strain of the church ran true in many hearts. Short, easily remembered statements could and clearly did function both as encapsulations of the truth for transmission to others, and also as identifiers of Christians among themselves. That is not to say, however, that there was no written message until the books of the New Testament came on the scene. Remember the debates of the Apostolic Council at Jerusalem, which may have taken place as early as fifteen years after the death of Christ. The outcome of that meeting was a specific letter to be sent to the Gentile churches with confirmation of the message to be spoken by its bearers (Acts 15:1-29, see esp. vv. 23-9, 22, with 30-32, and Acts 16:4-5). One notes, however, that the letter had its main impact in confirming an oral presentation of the Gospel.

The New Testament writings themselves have a part to play in the development. The Gospel records were written because there was a need, and, going by the preface to Acts, a demand, for a record of the historical facts upon which the faith was based. The epistles had a slightly different function. Some are for the encouragement of individuals, but many, including the bulk of Paul's writings, aim at setting out a correct statement of the faith, in some cases in specific opposition to error. Galatians is the obvious example.

When the Apostles were gone a major stage was reached. Where would the authority of any teaching lie? At the level of human organisation there was a need for a more summary presentation of the faith than was afforded by the New Testament. Paul did write some things which are hard to understand (2 Pet. 3:16). Some other expression of the truth was needed to summarise the common agreement of the church, both as to what he had meant as well as on other matters.

After the immediate New Testament times there were further developments. The writings of those we group as the Apostolic Fathers contain a number of the short summaries of much the same kind as

Paul may have used. There were also various creedal formulations of the faith being produced.[3] These at first had currency in different geographic areas, though some, for example what we call the Apostles' Creed, attained a wider authority. It is with the development of the organised church following upon its legalisation that statements authoritative for a whole church emerge.

Broadly there have been two major periods of confessional activity, one early and the other around the Reformation. Both these periods were marked by theological controversy.

The history of the early church is in a way quite astonishing, unless one remembers both the doctrine of original sin, and that God has an enemy. There was competition and dissension, faulty transmission of teaching and divergence of views. There was also deliberate invention or 'improvement' of the Gospel by those claiming special knowledge. The gnostics, objects of attack in Revelation, were but one group. Peter also says, running on from the words quoted above, that the 'ignorant and unstable twist to their own destruction' Paul's difficult passages, 'as they do the other scriptures' (2 Pet. 3:16). So the process was well established early. But once the Apostles and those who had known the Apostles died out, and perhaps their successors as well, there was a sprouting of variant doctrines with no-one to whom to appeal to set the record straight.

At first, of course, the church was an illegal organisation. There was, therefore, not the opportunity — one can say nothing about need — to consider the matter on a general basis. But once the church became official, and then compulsory, organisation was necessary. The church itself in measure copied the structures of the Roman Empire, especially as men trained in its administration came over into the new body. Organically the church required a generally accepted statement of orthodoxy for all the reasons which justify confessions. A simple statement of orthodoxy would identify believers, serve as a challenge to the outside world, and act as a test for those to whom the leadership of the church was entrusted. But it seems to have been the last purpose which was the main trigger. Truth had to be stated against error, and those embracing error had to be removed from power and influence. There was struggle, both theological and political, and then, some hundreds of years after Christ, the major creeds and confessions of the early church were arrived at. The Nicene Creed, Ephesus and Chalcedon, and so on, emerge from this period.

At the next wave of activity the problem was greater. The accumulated tradition and variant opinions of the Roman Catholic Church could not be dealt with simply. It followed that the Reformers had to produce statements and formulations which were in considerable detail, and these we tend to call 'confessions'. In the main they were statements, affirming what were held as truths by their framers.

---

3. J. N. D. Kelly, *Early Christian Creeds*, 3rd ed. London, Longmans, 1972.

But the Westminster Confession, for example, shows also another technique in the drafting of confessions. While one would always wish to be positive, there are times when the condemnation of untruth is the better way to proceed. It may not be sufficient to affirm a series of matters, error may have to be specifically labelled as such. The condemnation of the claim of the papacy to be the head of the church is one example (25:6).

The Reformation confessions were major theological documents. At the same time we must also recognise that there was a political element in the production of some at least of them. The English Parliament, for example, took the initiative in calling the Westminster Assembly, which produced the Westminster Confession of Faith and the Larger and Shorter Catechisms. It was also, by the way, that Parliament which asked for the proof verses to be added to the Confession, and this was done some months after the Assembly had agreed the text. This cuts the ground from the spurious argument that the Confession is *based* on sane texts which do not support its propositions. The Confession was agreed as a statement of the faith as understood by its compilers, and that statement does not depend for its authority upon the individual cited verses. The text is an encapsulation of agreement as to what the Bible teaches on the matters which it covers. While one may agree that some of the proof texts are inadequate, that does not destroy the statements to which they are attached.

But a confession of faith is only a human document. That of Westminster was negotiated among the participants in the Assembly. As it itself says, 'all councils may err' (31:4). The supreme judge in matters of faith is the Holy Spirit speaking in the Scripture (1:10). Therefore confessions of faith and any other synodical pronouncements 'are not to be made the rule of faith or practice, but to be used as an help in both' (31:4). To allege, as some have, that a confession has resulted in the Bible being interpreted by the confession and not the other way round, is, therefore, a very serious matter, suggesting deviation from *both* Scripture *and* Confession.

Some have suggested that to have such things as confessions is itself an act of unfaith. They would argue that our faith and practice should be governed simply by the Bible, and we should accept into our Christian community, including to positions of leadership, anyone who claims to be a Christian. For some a confession interferes with the authority of the Bible, or implies that the Bible is insufficient. For others the use of a confession as an identifier restricts the liberty of Christians. Others again consider the confessions with their differences divisive of the Body of Christ. Finally, there are some who consider that confessions restrict theological inquiry, freezing matters in the thought patterns and understandings of a long dead and manifestly imperfect society whose presuppositions and axioms we do not necessarily share.

I cannot go along with such arguments. I can see some force in them, but that relates to what I would call the abuse of a confession, not its proper use.

The substratum of these arguments seems to be an inarticulate dissatisfaction with reality. The fact is that denominations and congregations are human societies or institutions, which exist within society as a whole. As such there are questions of authority and control, of structure and responsibility, of property and income and expenditure which have to be dealt with in a way which is recognised within the legal system which is the context of each church. Into such matters confessions have been brought, for, since they serve to identify the common purpose and agreements, as well as sometimes the aims of a grouping, they can also be used to identify and demarcate that group for the purpose of society as a whole. They can be so used, and are so used not by external pressure, but by the will of the group, be it church or denomination, itself.

It remains as necessary as ever that the understanding of the gospel be stated. Only thus can like-minded folk freely associate together. Only thus will people contribute to the common cause. One of the hazards of theological plurality within a denomination is that ordinary members of the denomination will become reluctant to see their contributions financing ministries and undertakings which proceed on theological bases significantly different from that which they themselves hold. Their proper stewardship of their money will lead them to ensure that their givings are, in their opinion, well spent. If the gospel is about questions of eternal destiny, there is a limit to the variation on these matters which any organisation can stand. The Wolfe Report on the finances of the Church of Scotland provides material for the elaboration of these difficulties.[4]

Does this indicate a heresy hunt? By no means. There must be room within a denomination for variant views. The question, however, then becomes the point at which a variation is so extreme as to go beyond the lawful parameters. I think that was the point originally being raised within the Church of Scotland in the 1960's, before the matter was hijacked and converted into an attempt to displace the Westminster Confession. It has yet to be dealt with, and probably cannot be for all purposes by any doctrinal statement. The question will have to be determined in individual contested cases, whether a given variant is acceptable or not. I would oppose too much sensitivity on such matters. Historically it has been destructive of the witness of the Gospel. Sufficient attention has not always been given to the teaching of the parables of the Tares (Matt. 13:24-29, 36-43) and of the Drag-net (Matt. 25:47-50), and the search for a 'pure' church has become introverted, argumentative and unattractive to those outside

4. J. N. Wolfe and M. Pickford, *The Church of Scotland: An Economic Survey,* London, Chapman, 1980.

the church, thus failing in one of the primary Christian responsibilities, to win others for the Lord. At the same time churches have also been harmed by allowing continued membership to persons who clearly do not adhere to basic doctrines held by them. This confuses ordinary members, and provides ground for contempt by outsiders, again leading to the Gospel itself being ignored. Pragmatically (though arguably less importantly), the influence of the church even on secular matters is also thereby diminished. Why pay attention to those who claim some spiritual authority, but whose own house is manifestly in a mess?

Those who object to a confessional statement as restrictive seem to want the benefits of membership of the group which adheres to that statement without the restriction that the statement produces. Those who see a confession as divisive often seem to want to replace a form of church government which they have found uncongenial, and to introduce people with one set of beliefs to the ownership and use of church property and finances which were specifically contributed to an organisation holding a different set of beliefs.

This seems odd. Certainly if there is unanimity and identity between two groups there is no obstacle. Both, presumably, can agree to the confessional statement of the other. But in some cases one begins to have doubts as to what is really going on. The vehemence with which a confession is attacked can raise questions as to the integrity of an attacker who holds office within the church to whose confession he objects. Indeed, without going to the point of attack, it is observable that when a minister is known to hold views which do not square with the confession of his church, the status of all ministers is diminished. The world gleefully picks on what it construes as hypocrisy.

Am I therefore against all church union and the ecumenical process? By no means! But I would approach such matters from a somewhat different angle. It may well make no sense in organisational terms to have separate denominations operating within a given community where there is doctrinal agreement between them. But whether that situation calls for a union of the denominations, or for it to be agreed that one denomination take on the task of being the church in that area, is a different matter. And, apart from matters of doctrine, there are also questions of church government. Though I consider presbyterianism to be the form of church government most agreeable to the Word of God, and to afford benefits not found in other systems, to an extent such questions are matters of culture, and it is a nonsense to attempt to fuse divergent cultural traditions. 'That they may be one' is frequently quoted to argue the necessity of a united church, with a common pattern of government, or even, within certain new developments, of different patterns within some overall pattern. But the quotation runs on 'even as I and the Father are one', and there are, of course, three Persons in the Trinity. I see no duty for union in the way it is often presented, and rather marvel at the obtuseness of some who in practice despise the strengths of the organisations which have developed in their separate ways, or would willingly forfeit strength for a superficial unity. Some unions do make sense. Some are pursued for defective reasons of ideology.

But we are away from the matter of confessions. Confessions do enter into such questions, and are part of the reality which has to be addressed since they have been called into the way in which a state deals with a church. If one were to be setting up a new church or denomination, one would be free to do what one wished within the ordinary tenor of the law. Unfortunately a goodly part of discussions on the matter of confessions within existing denominations seems to assume a similar freedom of action, but without necessarily actually having it. In law a particular confession may be built into the identity of a denomination or a church. If such a present situation proves inconvenient, there is a temptation to elide the difficulty by an appeal to the Headship of Christ. It is argued that the church has an inherent power to do as it will with its doctrines since it is answerable only to its Lord.[5] The suggestion may be unwelcome that it could be unlawful, not to say immoral, to take the property and finances of an existing denomination, which were contributed on the basis of that denomination's particular identity as linked with, if not defined by, a particular confession. And yet it is the normal position in many legal systems that the property held by, or held in trust for, a congregation or a denomination, is held for the principles of the group concerned. It may be, of course, that one of those principles is the right to change its principles in response to new light if what was formerly professed is in some way deficient. Usually, however, modern views find deficiency to reside in undue precision as to the truths held. On matters of Heaven and Hell that precision would seem, however, to be desirable.

But even where there are legal constrictions, the law may be changed so that power to change becomes one of the principles. In Australia the law was changed to permit the formation of the Uniting Church of Australia, but the normal principle was also affirmed.[6] Again, other legal systems avoid the matter by refusing to get involved in internal church disputes. In the United States, the separation of church and state provided for by the First Article of the Bill of Rights means that the courts are wary in their approach to such matters, and ordinarily do not enter into such areas.[7]

But all that has to do with the institutional side of confessions, and perhaps, in the last analysis, the least important element of their

---

5. This was an argument in *Bannatyne* v *Lord Overtoun* (the Free Church case) (1904) 7 F. (H.L.)1; [1904] A.C. 515; R. L. Orr, ed., *The Free Church of Scotland Appeals, 1903-4*, Edinburgh, MacNiven and Wallace, 1904. It was rejected.
6. *Attorney-General for New South Wales (at the Relation of Neil MacLeod and Another)* v *Grant and Another* [1976] 10 A.L.R. 1; [1976] 135 C.L.R. 587; (1977) 51 A.L.J.R. 10.
7. *Watson* v *Jones* (1871) 13 Wall. 697; *Presbyterian Church* v *Mary Elizabeth Blue Hull Memorial Presbyterian Church* (1969) 393 U.S. 440.

utility. It ignores that important statement already quoted from the Westminster Confession. All councils may err, and therefore confessions of faith and any other synodical pronouncements 'are not to be made the rule of faith or practice, but to be used as an help in both' (cap. xxxi.4).

One of the things I have done in recent years has been to burrow through many of the Blue Books, the *Reports to the General Assembly of the Church of Scotland*. Occasionally a note would be sounded here and there, when the reports did report the feelings of the ordinary church members. It was a desire that they should be taught the faith, in deeper measure than they were then receiving.[8]

The consecutive preaching through the Scriptures is one way in which such a desire can be met, and is met at Gilcomston South Church. Familiarity with the Confession is another, and it has, with profit, been dealt with at our weekly meetings for Bible study. It therefore seems regrettable that the debate on the Confession showed that many elders, and even ministers, were not aware of its content. Given the content of ordination vows, that is puzzling, but, irrespective of that point, it remains true that confessions can be 'an help' in getting to know the faith. The phraseology is sometimes difficult, but the effort is worth it and has been made by many. Let no-one dismiss a confession merely because the language is said to be 'difficult'. C. S. Lewis points out that it is just not true that such language cannot be understood by ordinary people.[9] It can be, and is, though sometimes modern translations can help.[10]

To return to the Westminster Confession itself, it was the product of a number of men, sitting down together and seeking to put down on paper within a short compass their understanding of the Christian faith. It has its defects, not the least being the absence of a chapter on the Holy Spirit, and yet that Confession is very helpful and honest. It does not, for example, seek contortedly to harmonise Free Will and Predestination, but sets them both out as they may be found within the Bible itself. So often, on various matters, it provides a succinct statement, holding in tension major matters which others take pages to explicate for their professional readership. We ordinary members have neither the training nor the time to plough through the theologians. We appreciate the utility of the Confession, but without elevating it to an undue status. We, like its drafters, hold it subordinate to Scripture, and expect our ministers to teach us the faith. It is one of the marks of William Still's skill as a teacher of the faith that through his ministry so many have come to understand the truths contained in

---

8. Given the circumstances, I have also to report that there was usually coupled with that plea for teaching a request for shorter sermons, a request proven to be incompatible with the plea.

9. 'Before We Can Communicate', in C. S. Lewis, *Undeceptions: Essays on Theology and Ethics*, W. Hooper, ed., London, Bles, 1971, pp. 211-214.

10. A good modern translation of the American version of the Westminster Confession, with the U.S. variants, is D. Kelly, H. McClure and P. B. Rollinson, eds., *The Westminster Confession of Faith: A New Edition*, Greenwood, South Carolina, Attic Press, 1979.

the particular confession which historically is the strength of the Church of Scotland, and not only understood them, but allowed them to be 'an help' to the *practice* of the faith.

BUILDING THE CHURCH TODAY

GEORGE M. PHILIP

It is a basic principle of life and activity that if a man does not know what he is doing or is supposed to be doing it is most unlikely that he will achieve anything worthwhile. No matter how sincere, enthusiastic, gifted, intellectual or sound in theology he may be, unless he is quite clear about his objective, and the means to attain it he is unlikely to achieve much that is good. Indeed, he may well create something of a Frankenstein 'monster' which he neither likes nor desires, and is in fact unable to control. Almost inevitably he himself will be discouraged and disillusioned to the point of demoralisation. In the ecclesiastical realm he may soon be on the move to another area to try again. But if he is no clearer as to what he is supposed to be doing, and if he has no real consciousness of whose authority and direction he is working under, then the same confused issue will result. It is therefore of primary importance in all that is meant by 'building the church' to be clear about the nature and the inspiration of the God-given task.

When such a degree of confusion and uncertainty exists and has become established, it is all the more important to urge Christians, especially those called to full time ministry together with all who share in the on-going work and witness of the church, to think through clearly what it is they are called to do. There are many catch-words: 'mission', 'evangelism', 'outreach', 'impact', and the like, to say nothing of 'experiments' and 'new forms of worship'; but they can all too easily preoccupy the participants with what they themselves are doing at that immediate moment without ever allowing them to consider, let alone assess, exactly what it is they are supposed to be doing under God. No amount of change of methods or tools, and no amount of 'reports in depth', will ever prove effective unless there is a clear idea of the objective and an equally clear conviction that God has called us to do this very thing. There are many cynical voices saying that the church is crumbling (and so it is in terms of statistics and buildings) and that its day is finished. But over against that we have the affirmation of our Lord Jesus Christ that he will build his Church, and the gates of hell will not prevail against it. If that is his objective and we are called to be workers together with God (2 Cor.6:1), then we must see our work as 'building the church'. This must be our priority, and nothing must take its place. Clear conviction alone can give us continuing courage to go on and to keep going on.

When the church is spoken of today, especially in Scotland, people tend to think of the familiar ecclesiastical organisations with buildings of a certain kind in many strategic sites in cities and country. Sometimes those buildings that look far past their best do not give much evidence of significant or enthusiastic use by the people who claim membership. Even within the membership and life of the church the general idea is of a large and complicated business venture, dealing with religious and social matters, with its organisation, structure and committees, all overshadowed by the central church offices, 'the powers that be' who are always asking for money and telling congregations what they may or may not do. Until the present generation, during which the pattern has altered significantly, the church was very much the place people went to because their parents and grandparents went there before them, and the 'habit' of church-going was considered a proper thing, especially for the children! However, with the change in the social climate, the ascendancy of humanist philosophy, the emphasis on secularism, and the constant flow and change in the economic situation leading to people moving more frequently, contact is lost with the 'family church', the church they went to (or did not go to) for baptisms, marriages and funerals. The 'church' becomes either a place in some other area, a memory of long ago that creates a degree of wistfulness, or a place locally where everyone is a stranger, a place to which fewer and fewer people seem to go, especially of the younger generation. To try to build a church in a situation and atmosphere like this appears as a hopeless task, unless there is a clear concept of what the church really is and can be, and a conviction that God himself has called his people together for this purpose.

If God desires to gather a people to himself it is both sad and significant that generally speaking, even among those who profess to be evangelical, biblical believers, there is a strange lack of interest in the doctrine of the church. Individualism has become dominant, a sense of duty is almost regarded as a sign of weakness, and any suggestion of discipline or rebuke,and in some cases even exhortation can meet with resentment. This stems in great part from a devaluing of the ministry as a God-ordained office, given for the good of God's people. It is no surprise that preaching is also lightly regarded almost as an 'extra', if not a kind of 'performance' to be liked or enjoyed or criticised and refused. Few seem to see that in the preaching and hearing of the Word of God there is in fact the experience of a divine encounter, whereby men and women are made wise unto salvation, fed by the Bread of God and built up in their most holy faith.

It is both strange and sad that the terms 'church planting' and 'church building' are to a great extent confined to the overseas missionary work of the church, and to that part of overseas mission undertaken by the interdenominational societies. The major denominations apparently tend to assume that the church is there, and that what has been will go on being. Our society is increasingly materialistic in its philosophy and is becoming increasingly multi-racial, with a variety of cultural patterns and practices. If the Christian gospel is to survive, let alone progress, then churches must be built that will stand no matter what happens. Such churches must be clear, convinced and instructed in the fundamentals of the faith; churches that will not be just religious institutions, but family homes for believers together with their children of all ages.

Of course we must not fall into the snare of narrowing down our vision of the church to a merely local and congregational concept. That would cause us to be preoccupied with the hazards, the limits and the disappointments of our own situation, without having the encouragement of being aware that we are part of one glorious, universal work of the living God. It is necessary to remind ourselves constantly of both the geographical and historical nature of the church. Paul greeted the congregation at Corinth and made them aware of all that they were and all that they shared together with all those in every place who call on the name of the Lord (1 Cor.1:2). This is the church we are part of, no matter how small and seemingly insignificant our local work may be. This is what we are, no matter how large, important and well recognised our own congregation may be. We are a part, only a part, but a glorious part. The very fact that we are there at all is entirely due to the gracious working of God's Spirit through his Word. It is God alone who works salvation. It is God alone who gives the increase (1 Cor.3:6,7). Apart from him we can do nothing (1 John 15:4,5). It is Christ who builds the church and who adds to it those who are being saved (Acts 2:47).

We must also grasp the historical dimension of the building of the church. The work neither begins nor ends with us. Other men have laboured and we have entered into their labours (John 4:37,38). We can never be free from the sense of debt we owe to those who have gone before us. Their work may not have been perfect, and at times what they accomplished and built may have subsequently lapsed from its spiritual freshness and dynamic. But the fact remains that our predecessors fought battles, laid foundations and formulated the great confessions and creeds whereby through dark ages the substance of the faith was preserved for following generations. Of course, we in our generation also create situations and leave legacies which will have to be lived with for good or ill by those who come after us. This is indeed a tremendous responsibility which should always challenge and direct us in our part of building the church. But we must never lose sight of the immense privilege it is to be part of the work and witness of the church of Christ in its on-going life down through the generations of history. This is something that gives dignity to our persons and our work. We are lifted up from obscurity and irrelevance, and given the honour and function of being workers together with God.

It is here that we are compelled to recognise that in the economy of God the church is, and must ever be, distinct from the world. It is different from the world both in its nature and its destiny. There is nothing in Scripture to cause us to believe that the created world as we know it is going to last for ever. Indeed, we are told that the heavens and the earth as we now know them will pass away. Both the words and the imagery used to declare this seem to signify a great cataclysmic end to creation's history, not by the agency of man nor by his scientific ingenuity, either deliberately or accidentally, but by the specific design of God. In the plan of God when this little planet earth has served the purpose for which it was brought into being, it will pass away. But the church is spoken of as eternal. Its destiny is in eternity, where it will be a glorious church without spot or blemish or any such thing (Eph.5:25-27). It is only in the world to come that the church will be seen as she really is destined to be, the glorious, spotless bride of Christ.

The church is not a voluntary society (of which there are many in the world doing good and beneficial work for humanity) which people may or may not join according to inclination or conviction. The church is made up of all those who believed on the Lord Jesus Christ as Saviour, who have been born anew of the Spirit of God, who have been made members of the family of God and who are called to his eternal glory (2 Peter 1:3). Inasmuch as they are members of Christ they are members of his body, which is the church, and they are members one of another. The church is a living spiritual organism not a human organisation. It is not a building, nor a conglomerate of buildings, made of stone and lime, but one spiritual building made of living stones (1 Peter 2:5) built together to form a habitation of God by the Spirit.

To speak of God dwelling amongst his people, not ashamed to be called their God, and enjoying their company as well as receiving their worship and their glad service is indeed a glorious and moving concept. It corresponds well with the affirmation in the Shorter Catechism that the chief end of man is to glorify God and to enjoy him both now and for ever. This points to the fact that true spiritual religion is not a burdensome thing of dry duty, and mental and emotional frustration. We are not dealing with that travesty of Christ, Swinburn's 'pale Galilean' who causes the whole world to grow grey under his influence. We are dealing with the One who said that he had come in order that we might have life to the full. When we are building churches we are not really concerned with structures but rather with family homes where people of all ages, backgrounds and capacities become, through Christ, members of the household of God, God's fireside family (Eph. 2:19). It is the God of salvation who presides over the family and his presence with his people is the very breath of life whereby we have fellowship with the Father and with his Son Jesus Christ and consequently fellowship with one another.

Since this is so, 'going to church', which so many pre-judge as dull in the extreme, is a most significant exercise. There is a tremendous therapy mentally, psychologically and spiritually in being part of a congregation of God's people at worship. The presence of God among his own ransomed people and the activity of the Spirit of God in life-giving and life-sweetening grace and power, in and through every constituent part of the service, make every such gathering an occasion of profound spiritual significance. An essential and central part of that worship is the preaching and hearing of the Word of God. As people are taught by the Word, corrected, cautioned, inspired and fed by it, then the whole pattern of their thinking is moulded by it so that they begin to think wholesomely and in Scriptural and spiritual categories. This is the beginning of creative Christian service and the beginning of a true understanding of the work of God.

This does not in any sense picture the church as an escape ghetto for pious Christians who cannot cope with the real world. Real 'spiritual homes' will always be frequented by enquirers, seekers, prodigals, rebels and a whole host of people with a variety of hurts, hopes, fears and needs. In a society that is cruelly and even sadistically impersonal, a society which causes people to feel 'rootless', there is a basic 'attraction' to a place and a people where there is an awareness of life and peace, hope and purpose. In this sense the building of the church is both the essence and power of evangelism and outreach. Think of how the people gathered to Jesus, and how, even when he sought solitude, he could not be hid (Mark 7:24). Think of how the whole of the neighbourhood (including the critics) gathered to John the Baptist as a result of his radical preaching of repentance. By the power of the Holy Spirit there was 'inflow' rather than frantic, organised outreach. Think of the marvellous words in the prophecy of Zechariah telling of a day when people from far and near would say, 'Let us go with you, because we have heard that God is with you.' (Zech.8:23). This is the kind of church we need to build. But how is it to be done?

There has to be clear thinking on the levels of procedure and practice. All too often various denominations have 'built a church' in a certain area. That is, they have erected a building or a complex of buildings and then have set about looking for people to come to them. What is happening is further confused in the mid 1980's by the enthusiasm for a multi-purpose building used not only by several denominations but by social service and community authorities. This can lead to a bustle of activity and an impression of success and ever-increasing influence. No doubt in terms of community service such a 'centre' is both justified and valuable and we have no desire to criticise or devalue social work. The church does a great deal of it and inspires many others to do the same. Where there is need there must be care and it must not be on the lowest level of a 'cup of cold water' in Jesus' name. Responsibilities of service have to be fulfilled willingly but they are not the same as, nor a substitute for, the building of the church. The church in biblical terms is a God-centred, God-worshipping, God-learning and God-serving, God-glorifying family of people who are one in Christ because they have believed the Gospel and have been born into the family of God.

The church belongs to Christ and is redeemed by Christ, washed by Christ, ministered to by Christ, nurtured and fed by Christ, built up and matured by Christ until all believers grow together to the measure of the stature of the fulness of Christ. Within this gathered unity and never apart from it individualism finds its true and safe expression. The members of the body of Christ are unique in themselves, not only allowed but required to be themselves in their individual capacities and gifts in order that they might be effective 'joints and sinews' (Eph.4:16; Col.2:19) whereby the body functions in obedience to and service of its Head, who is Christ. In all its developments, in all its growth to maturity, and in all its costly service the church is warmed by the love of Christ and reassured by the fact that Christ rules over all things in the interest of the Church (Eph.1:22).

The church is not yet complete, it is still being built by Christ himself and the gates of hell can neither prevent the building nor can they stand against the church. We do wrong and rob ourselves of both thrill and peace when we begin to think of the church as being on the defensive. Through the whole of the Old Testament we read of the mighty hand of God working for the protection, the victory and the sanctification of His people. His purposes are sure and even though his ways are mysterious and past finding out they are always effective. In the New Testament we have the Gospel accounts of the total victory of Christ in his death and resurrection, and in the Epistles we have the account of on-going work of the gospel and the building of the church on the foundation of the prophets and apostles, Jesus Christ himself being the head corner-stone. The whole story of the New Testament is diffused with a sense of confidence and assurance. In every generation the men and women who are in Christ, and therefore who are the church, are urged to be steadfast, unmoveable, always abounding in the work of the Lord because their labour is not in vain in the Lord (1 Cor.15:58).

What then is the labour that must be the essence of building the church? The contemporary church situation would give a variety of answers ranging through routine visitation, concentration on youth work, getting involved in socio-political issues affecting the parish and the nation, campaigns against evils in other countries and livening up services by way of music, drama and dancing as part of worship. There are even those who would advocate getting rid of the Bible, its truths and standards: a desire expressed on a television interview by a minister who described the New Testament Gospels as a 'collection of grossly exaggerated stories'. But, when you read the New Testament, you discover that the church was a preaching church and the pattern of its ministry was reasoning out of the Scriptures. The spiritual debility of the church in our generation stems from its neglect of the Scriptures, a neglect that is becoming recognised, as is evident from the increasing emphasis on the need for education within the church, starting with the eldership, in order to dispel the ignorance of Scripture and Christian doctrine. An example of this ignorance was seen in a young, go-ahead business man, an elder in the Kirk, who stated, 'What I like about the story of the Cross is that there is no theology in it.' If that is symptomatic of the understanding of the eldership then it is little wonder that the church is crumbling rather than being built.

It would be wrong to suggest that there is not concern in the church. There *is* concern and a great deal of energy and ingenuity are being addressed to remedying the situation. But by and large the route being followed is one of reorganisation on every level from administration, through new forms of worship, new patterns for raising Christian liberality, to new schemes of teaching material for all ages. But the sheer volume of changes and experiments is self-defeating. This has always been the case. Consider the following quotation from the Satyricon of Petronius Arbiter, A.D.66:

> We trained hard — but it seemed that every time we were beginning to form up into teams, we would be reorganised. I was to learn later in life that we tend to meet any new situation by reorganising, and a wonderful method it can be for creating the illusion of progress while producing confusion, inefficiency and demoralisation.

The illusion of progress created by activity of the kind mentioned above is the very thing that keeps the church from recognising that by and large it is failing to get down to the business of building the church. The distraction is subtle. It is right and proper to emphasise that the gospel must be applied to every part of human life, personal and social. No-one can possibly disagree with that. But the *application* of the gospel is not the explanation of the gospel and should not precede it. The imperative declaration of the message of salvation, the forgiveness of sins, and the power of Christ to transform and deliver sinners from their guilt and their condition must come before the application of that truth to life. If the order is reversed and the preaching of the gospel of salvation is either displaced or assumed (or even denied) then we first qualify the message, then ignore it and finally lose it. This is the present national situation. By and large people do not know that there is a gospel, that there is a need for salvation and that sinners need to be reconciled to God. To a great extent people assume that they and everyone else are in some way 'Christian' and that all go to heaven in the end. If people are given the impression that all go to heaven no matter how they have ignored God and Christ, then they will obviously take the attitude that there is no great need to bother about salvation and in consequence the church is regarded as irrevelant or at best an interesting activity for those so inclined, especially women and children.

Think of the apostolic situation. It was a society living under totalitarian military rule. It was marked by entrenched materialism and social breakdown with the inevitable disintegration of marriage and family life. It was evident that its cultural achievements were past their peak and there were many evidences of emergent demonism. There was a tremendous ignorance of the truth of God, as evidenced by the altar in Athens to 'The Unknown God'. In that situation the apostles and missionaries, armed with the Scriptures and with a burning desire to make Christ known, turned the world upside down.

They were convinced about their message and they laid out the truth of Scripture systematically. They were equally convinced that their methods were not carnal or worldly and they made no attempt to copy the patterns and procedures of society. Their weapon was the Scriptures and they had confidence in them and in the God who had given them. The fruit of their work was the building of the church.

If we consider the accounts of apostles' preaching in the Acts of the Apostles as they opened up the Scriptures and affirmed the truths concerning the person and work of Christ in his death and resurrection; and if we consider the comprehensive nature and the spiritual depth of the teaching of the Epistles, letters sent in the first instance to comparatively new Christians and newly established congregations that were still feeling their way, then we have a marvellous example of the kind of ministry by which salvation is heralded and the church built in an unfriendly, antagonistic and needy society. We have also a tremendous challenge and a glorious encouragement to go and to do the very same thing in the very same way in our own generation, getting down to the systematic preaching of the Word of God, expounding and applying it in such a way that all who hear will know beyond any shadow of doubt that we both believe it and are prepared to live by it.

This deliberate commitment to the preaching of the Word of God, going through Old and New Testaments book by book, chapter by chapter, verse by verse where necessary, is the 'experiment' which simply has it been tried by the generality of the church over the past forty years. The ignorance of the Scriptures inside the church and the apparent distaste for coming to grips with the basic doctrines of salvation and life give manifest evidence of this appalling neglect. It is not a situation that can be rectified on the basis of conference and training week-ends, valuable as these may be at times. Nor is it a situation to be rectified by simply reading books and pamphlets, or by personal Bible study, or by means of small group discussions, however valuable these may be. The root of the remedy lies in the pulpits of individual congregations with the Word of God being fully preached, holding back nothing that is profitable. But this is not a case of cold, clinical statements of Biblical truth, nor an obsessive concern to have every theological sentence exactly formulated. Such a manner of preaching tends to cause people either to switch off because they have heard it all before or to make them look for doctrinal inaccuracies, and so fail to hear the Word of God. The Scriptures must be unfolded, preached and applied as the very bread of God to feed the souls of the people. It is the Word of God for life, every aspect of life, and the preacher has the responsibility to show the people how comprehensively this Word applies to them.

Not all will agree that working through books of the Bible, balancing Old and New Testament, giving full place to the Gospel narratives, and tackling epistles such as Romans at regular intervals, is necessarily the best way. But the one thing that must be done is to deal with all the Scriptures and so preserve a true balance of Biblical truth for feeding, guiding and instructing the flock of God, enabling them to grow up into Christ ready for sacrificial service, and at the same time equipping them to discern and to stand against all the false messages that riddle and corrupt present-day society. It can only be described as tragedy that there are men in the ministry for many years who have never once, for example, led their people right through even one of the Gospels, or through the glories of Paul's Letter to the Romans, or for that matter led them through a systematic study of the Apostles' Creed, let alone the Westminster Confession of Faith.

It is recorded in Scripture that an educated man from Ethiopia was reading his scroll of Isaiah's prophecy when Philip, led by the Spirit of God, came to him and asked if he understood what he was reading and of whom the Scriptures spoke. His reply, 'How can I understand except someone teaches me?' is a heart-cry that is echoed many times in our own generation. To ignore that cry or to fail to answer it by presenting dry husks rather than the bread of God, is to fail in what Jesus commanded, 'Feed my sheep'. It is recorded in the Old Testament that a revival of true religion in the time of Josiah took place as a direct result of the re-discovery of the Word of God in the House of God. A church that has lost the Bible is a church that has nothing to say that will be of saving help to society. But a church built on the Word of God is a church that will know what it believes. It will never be an impersonal religious gathering but will grow to be a family and a fellowship whose hunger will be both met and yet also stimulated by the good Word of God. It will bring into being churches that are marked by a sense of the presence of God, churches that are centred on the person of the Lord Jesus Christ. In a lost and lonely generation that is increasingly frightened because there is nothing to live for, nothing to be sure about, nowhere to go and indeed no signposts to show the way, there will gather again to Jesus all the lame and the blind, the needy and the oppressed. When such find a Saviour and learn his love and gracious power they will not only rejoice, they will teach their children and their children's children after them, and the church will go on being built.

All that has been said in this article has been the foundation and inspiration of a systematic ministry of the Word of God in the same congregation for nearly thirty years. In measure at least it has proved itself, as even its critics would concede. These basic principles of ministry and the vision of its possibilities were learned by sitting under such a ministry in Gilcomston South Church, Aberdeen for six years. These decades of experience have brought the conviction that a truly Biblical ministry is the ideal and creative context for pastoral counselling, not least because it makes people willing to be helped and brings them under the gracious influence of both Word and worship. Systematic preaching is demanding. It calls for a rigorous ordering of priorities and an equally rigorous refusal of distractions. But once a man sees the true glory of the on-going work of the local congregation and is prepared under God to give himself to it with gladness of heart, that man will know he has in very truth the privilege of being a fellow-labourer with God in the building of the church.

THE REFORMED DOCTRINE OF SONSHIP

SINCLAIR B. FERGUSON

In his famous (and controversial) William Cunningham Lectures entitled *The Fatherhood of God,* R. S. Candlish expressed his purpose in these words:

> My object is chiefly a practical one. It is to bring out the import and bearing of the Scriptural doctrine respecting the Fatherhood of God as an influential element in Christian experience.[1]

The purpose of this essay is to look at the same relationship between Christian experience and the Fatherhood of God, but to do so from a different perspective, namely from the standpoint of the Christian's sonship. Four areas will be discussed briefly: the development and demise of the doctrine in Christian theology; the centrality of the doctrine in biblical theology; its usefulness as a perspective on the nature of salvation; the illumination it yields for our relationship with God.

Sonship: Development and Demise of a Doctrine

If one paints the history of theology with a broad brush, it is clear that neither the early nor the mediaeval church expressed much interest in the idea of the Christian life as a life of *sonship.* The controversies of both periods lay elsewhere. Furthermore, the methods of biblical interpretation adopted were virtually incapable of isolating sonship as a central theme in biblical theology. In the case of mediaeval theology, with its development of an elongated *ordo salutis,* its distinction between unformed faith and faith formed by love *(fides informis; fides formata charitate),* its emphasis on penance, purgatory and the place of indulgences, the doctrine of the ordinary Christian as a child of God entitled to all the privileges and joys of fellowship with a loving Father, would have had devastating effects.[2]

Devastating effects did occur, of course, in the Reformation. But it was Luther's doctrine of justification by faith which produced them. However, in the context of this essay, it needs to be said that Luther's stress on justification was at the expense of emphasising the privilege of sonship. Sonship, insofar as it is discussed, is subservient to justification. At best it is the *seal* of justification. The recognition that sonship is 'the apex of redemptive grace and privilege',[3] higher in

1. R. S. Candlish, *The Fatherhood of God.* Edinburgh 1864, p. 103.
2. Still a valuable popular introduction to this is to be found in T. M. Lindsay, *History of the Reformation,* Edinburgh 1906, I, pp. 216-227.
3. J. Murray, *Collected Writings* Edinburgh, 1977, 2, p. 233.

nature than justification, is one to which Luther would probably not have warmed!

It was left to the reformed theological tradition, following the lead of Calvin, to recover this biblical emphasis. Even within that tradition, the emphasis has appeared somewhat spasmodically.

Students of Calvin's theology have too rarely recognised how important the concept of sonship was to his understanding of the Christian life. (We do not readily adjust to the notion that the young man who was known by his classmates as 'the accusative case' later revelled in the idea of being God's child!) While there is no separate chapter on sonship in the *Institutes, adoptio* (sonship) is one of the expressions by which he most frequently designates the idea of being a Christian. He does not treat sonship as a separate *locus* of theology precisely because it is a concept which undergirds everything he writes.

Calvin's *Institutes* began life as what the title page called a *summa pietatis* (sum of piety). But for Calvin, piety meant recognising that our lives are nourished by God's *Fatherly* care;[4] it meant knowing oneself to be a child of God. Similarly, Calvin saw the purpose of the incarnation and atonement to be the adoption of Christians.[5] Consequently, the 'first title' of the Spirit is 'Spirit of adoption'.[6] The knowledge of adoption is the believer's consolation in suffering.[7] It is no surprise then, to the reader of the *Institutes,* to encounter Calvin at his most eloquent when he comes to expound the phrase 'Our Father' in the Lord's Prayer.[8] As Émile Doumergue has succinctly expressed it, for Calvin 'It is the knowledge of his Fatherly love that is the true knowledge of God'.[9]

Despite occasional statements to the contrary, this emphasis of Calvin was kept alive within the Puritan tradition. William Ames' famous lectures in Leyden in 1620-22, later to be published as his *Marrow of Sacred Divinity,*[10] contained an entire section on adoption, and in characteristically Puritan fashion offered a series of twenty-seven different points of exposition. Further discussion took place in the writings of other Puritans, perhaps most notably in the sensitive exposition of the Independent theologian, John Owen.[11] Significantly, for Owen, the doctrine of adoption was intimately related to the idea of communion and fellowship with God.

Paradoxically to those who regard the Westminster Confession of Faith as a document breathing all too little of the fresh air of Calvin's theology, it is in the Westminster Confession (followed by its cousins,

4. J. Calvin, *Institutes of the Christian Religion,* I.ii.1.
5. *Ibid.,* II.xii. 2, cf. II.xiv.5-6.
6. *Ibid.,* III.i.3.
7. *Ibid.,* III.viii.8.
8. *Ibid.,* III.xxi.7.
9. Émile Doumergue, *Jean Calvin: Les hommes et les choses de son temps,* Lausanne, 1910, IV, pp. 90-1. It is significant that Doumergue devotes several pages in his exposition of Calvin's doctrine of God to the idea of God as Father.
10. The Latin edition appeared in 1623 and was later followed by an English edition in 1638.
11. John Owen, *Collected Works* ed. W. H. Goold, Edinburgh, 1850-53, 2, pp. 207-222.

the Independent *Savoy Declaration of Faith and Order* and the Baptist London or Philadelphia *Confession of Faith*) that the doctrine of adoption is given a separate chapter in a confession of the Christian Church. Perhaps more than anything else it is the presence of this brief chapter which has kept alive within Presbyterianism (particularly in Scotland and the Southern Presbyterian Church in the U.S.A.) the significance of sonship in the life of faith.

The doctrine of adoption suffered considerable demise in later years. The view that it was simply the 'positive side' of justification — Luther's rather than Calvin's view — never really died. It is to be found in some of the classical expositions of theology in the reformed tradition. Charles Hodge remains silent on the theme of adoption in his *Systematic Theology*[12]. His remarkable contemporary, R. L. Dabney (right-hand man to none other than 'Stonewall' Jackson!) devoted some twenty-two lines only to it in his *Lectures in Systematic Theology*.[13] Despite the efforts of Candlish in Scotland and such Southern Presbyterians as J. L. Girardeau, in his *Discussion of Theological Questions* and R. A. Webb, in his somewhat disappointing *Reformed Doctrine of Adoption*, sonship was denied the place in systematic theology which biblical teaching would suggest it merited.

The reason for its demise in the reformed theological tradition may be traced back to the profound influence on English-speaking reformed theology of Turretin's monumental *Theological Institutes*. Turretin did give consideration to the question of sonship, but did so by posing the question 'What is the adoption which is given to us in justification?'[14] The form in which the question was asked assured the continuing subservience of adoption to justification, and its secondary rather than climactic position in theological thinking. Turretin answered his own question in these terms:

> Adoption is included in justification as a part, which with the remission of sins constitutes the whole of this benefit; nor can it be distinguished from adoption.[15]

Turretin did have the great merit of linking Christian liberty to the idea of adoption, but the formulation he gave to the relation between justification and adoption became the bench-mark for most later expositions.

This long-standing tradition, linked with the influence of nineteenth century Liberalism's emphasis on the universal Fatherhood of God and the corresponding universal sonship and brotherhood of man might have seemed to sound the death-knell of the doctrine of adoption. Evangelical teaching in general fought shy of the employ-

---

12. C. Hodge, *Systematic Theology*, 1872-3, r.i. London, 1960, vol. III.
13. R. L. Dabney, *Lectures in Systematic Theology*, Richmond 1878, p. 627. Cf. also L. Berkhof, *Systematic Theology*, Grand Rapids 1941), pp. 515-6.
14. F. Turretin, *Opera*, Edinburgh 1847, II. p. 585: 'Quod sit adoptio quae nobis in justificatione datur? I. Altera pars justificatione est adoptio.'
15. *Ibid.*

ment of language (Fatherhood of God, sonship of man) which had become hallmarks of Liberalism and Universalism.

Voices have, however, cried in the wilderness. In addition to Candlish, Girardeau and Webb, honourable mention must be made of the two Baptist theologians John Gill[16] and James Petigru Boyce.[17] More recently John Murray[18] and James I. Packer[19] have lent their weight to a recovery of the doctrine of sonship. Perhaps more than any other influence, the impact of biblical theology on systematic theology has demanded a reorientation of soteriology towards the concept of sonship. The doctrine may therefore be on the verge of a long-awaited reinstatement to the position it occupied in Calvin's thought, one which pervades the whole ethos of the Christian life.

The Centrality of Sonship in Biblical Doctrine

There are two ways in which the centrality of sonship is evident in Scripture:

(i) In the programmatic texts of the New Testament it is commonplace to discover an emphasis on sonship. When the writers discuss the flow of God's plan, from election through the flow of the history of redemption, the purpose of the incarnation and the accomplishments of the atonement, sonship is a central focus. The new covenant introduces the church to a new experience of sonship; the work of the Spirit in conforming us to Christ has sonship in view — Christ is to be the firstborn among many brothers (see, for example, Gal. 3:26-4:7; Eph. 1:3-6; Rom. 8:28-31; Heb. 2:10-18).

(ii) In the wider context of biblical theology, sonship is stressed in three distinct ways:

(a) Sonship is the focus of creation. Reformed theologians and exegetes have debated whether Adam in creation was a son of God or was intended to be adopted as a son following a period of testing in Eden. The state of the question has rested a good deal on whether Luke 3:38 gives positive encouragement to think of Adam as the *created* son of God. More recently Jeremias has underlined the significance of the Adam-Christ parallel which follows the announcement of Luke 3:38, as the Last Adam is exposed to the wilderness temptations as the Son of God. The case for thinking of Adam's relationship to God as *filial* in nature is strengthened by two considerations: the lavishness of the provision made for him, in Genesis 2 (a father's love expressed for his son); the intimate connection between sonship and image in Genesis 1:26-8 and Genesis 5:1-3.

---

16. John Gill, *Body of Divinity*, London 1769-70, Book VI, chap. 9.
17. James Petigru Boyce, *Abstract of Systematic Theology*, 1887. See especially his judicious criticisms of other reformed theologians on pp. 404-409.
18. J. Murray, *Redemption — Accomplished and Applied*, Grand Rapids, 1955, pp. 132-140; *Collected Writings*, 2, pp. 223-234.
19. J. I. Packer, *Knowing God*, London 1973, pp. 223-257.

In either case — whether Adam was created as a child of God or to enter into the enjoyment of sonship — the filial relation lies at the heart of God's creating purposes.

(b) Sonship is the pattern of redemption. When God redeems his people in the Old Testament, it is the filial model which most eloquently describes the relationship between the Lord and his people. Moses tells Pharaoh that God's word is 'Israel is my firstborn son, and I told you "Let my son go, so he may worship me" but you refused to let him go; so I will kill your firstborn son' (Ex. 4:22-3). The basis for Moses later upbraiding the people is precisely this: 'Is he not your Father, your Creator, who made you and formed you?' (Deut. 32:6). Again the Father-son metaphor appears in the exquisite picture of the Exodus in Deuteronomy 1:31: 'You saw how the Lord your God carried you, as a father carries his son, all the way you went until you reached this place'.

This is what Paul refers to as 'the adoption as sons' (Rom. 9:4). Adoption is not itself an Old Testament concept.[20] But the Roman legal metaphor which Paul borrowed from the world in which he lived admirably summarised the *nature* of the sonship unveiled by the Old Testament and brought to fulfilment in Jesus Christ. Yet even the Old Testament pictures the salvation of God's people in language which is tantamount to adoption:

> This is what the Sovereign Lord says to Jerusalem: Your ancestry and birth were in the land of the Canaanites; your father was an Amorite and your mother a Hittite. On the day you were born your cord was not cut, nor were you washed with water to make you clean, nor were you rubbed with salt or wrapped in cloth. No one looked on you with pity or had compassion enough to do any of these things for you. Rather you were thrown out into the open field, for on the day you were born you were despised.
> Then I passed by and saw you kicking about in your blood, and as you lay there in your blood I said to you, 'live!' I made you grow like a plant of the field. You grew up and developed . . . .
> Later I passed by, and when I looked at you and saw that you were old enough for love, I spread the corner of my garment over you and covered your nakedness. I gave you my solemn oath and entered into covenant with you, declares the Sovereign Lord, and you became mine.
> Ezekiel 16:3-8

Salvation is God taking the fondling child and bringing it into a new family relationship altogether. It is adoption into the covenant of love.

(c) Sonship is also the goal of restoration. The entire process of sanctification, leading to the final restoration of glorification, is intended to bring to perfection our sonship to the Father. We are being transformed into the likeness of Christ in order that he might be the firstborn of many brothers (Rom. 8:29). This is the 'One, far-off, divine event, to which the whole creation moves' (Tennyson). But it is

20. See F. Lyall, *Slaves, Citizens and Sons: Legal metaphors in the Epistles,* Grand Rapids 1984, pp. 67-99.

not so far-off from the biblical point of view. Already we are sons of God (1 Jn. 3:1-3). It does not yet appear what we shall be. But even now the creation 'stands on tiptoe' waiting to see the sons of God 'come into their own' (Rom. 8:19 cf. J. B. Phillips translation). The process of sanctification is, in essence, the reproduction of the family-likeness in the people of God; it involves us being transformed to be more and more like the Elder Brother, because he is the express likeness of the Father.

We might therefore summarise the grace of the gospel by saying that it involves adoption into the family of God, with the corresponding process of ridding us of the influences of our former family and more and more remaking us to conform to the Incarnate Son.

Sonship as an Organising Principle for Understanding Salvation

The question of the most appropriate model by which to understand salvation has been much debated in reformed theology. It has been characteristic, for example, for reformed theology to make considerable use of the idea of ordered experience *(ordo salutis)*. As we have already noted, characteristic of Lutheran theology has been the principle of justification.

It is probably an error of some magnitude to insist that only one principle should be employed to unify one's understanding of the nature of salvation. Scripture provides us with various models, of which justification is but one. Sonship may well be proposed as another.

Any organising principle for the doctrine of salvation must meet certain important biblical tests: Does it convey the covenantal perspective of the Bible? Does it arise out of the flow of redemptive history? Is it eschatological in nature (that is, does it express the 'already/not yet' tension which is so characteristic of the New Testament's view of present Christian existence)? Does it centre on Jesus Christ?

Sonship meets each of these tests in a satisfactory manner. It is a covenantal concept. Simply expressed, biblical covenants bind individuals to the family. God's covenant binds men and women to his family as his children. It is a blood covenant making Christians 'blood-brothers'. Notice the extent to which the events surrounding the covenant of the Exodus are described in terms of God establishing the Father-son relationship (Deut. 1:31; Jer. 31:9; Hos. 11:1 etc.).

But sonship is also a concept through which the development of salvation in biblical history is encapsulated. It does not 'flatten out' the contours of redemptive history. In the Old Testament period (until Pentecost), God's people are indeed his children. But they are as yet under age; they have not been brought to mature sonship. They are heirs in their minority. But now, by contrast, we have 'come of age' in the era of the Spirit of sonship. This is the trend of thought in Paul's argument in Galatians 3:23-4:7. Not only so, but we look forward to yet fuller dimensions of the experience of sonship (1 Jn. 3:1-3). It does not yet appear what we shall be!

Consequently, sonship is characterised *now* by the tension between what has *already* been accomplished for us in Christ and what is *yet to be* accomplished. We already possess the adoption as sons and the presence of the Spirit of adoption. But precisely because of that, we long for its consummation. Those who have the Spirit of adoption (the 'firstfruits of the Spirit') *groan*, says Paul (Rom. 8:23). Why? Because enjoying the privileges of sons now, we anticipate the glorious liberty of sons in the future when we receive the 'adoption as sons' which Paul describes variously as 'the redemption of our bodies' and 'the glorious freedom of the children of God' and a 'share in his glory' (Rom. 8:23, 21, 19).

Sonship, then, has a retrospective and a prospective dimension. It recognises what has already been accomplished: we have been adopted into God's family and experience the access and liberty of grace. But it also recognises that more is still to be accomplished: we look forward to eschatological adoption, and the access and liberty of glory. The omega-point of Christian experience has not yet come for us. But it will; the fact that we are already children of God is the guarantee.

Sonship, however, is also centred in Jesus Christ. It is because he has entered our family that we enter the family of God (Heb. 2:5-18). Only because he is not ashamed to call us brothers may we call his Father, 'our Father' (cf. Jn. 20:17). Indeed it can be argued that in Pauline thought the resurrection of Christ is viewed as his 'adoption'[21] — not in the sense that he became Son of God in the resurrection, but insofar as he was 'marked out as the Son of God with power through the resurrection' (Rom. 1:4). He was 'firstborn from the dead', brought into the family of the new age by resurrection. Through union with Christ, in which we are 'raised into newness of life', we too are adopted into that family. It is, therefore, only in Christ, in the family fellowship we have with him, that we are adopted children of God. He has not left us orphans, after all (Jn. 14:18). He has given us the Spirit of sons (Rom. 8:15).

The biblical doctrine of sonship, therefore, well summarises the whole of the life of the Christian in relation to God.

Sonship and the Character of God

R. S. Candlish spoke of the doctrine of the Fatherhood of God as an 'influential element in Christian experience'. We, likewise, studying the same relationship from the opposite end as it were, may say that sonship is an influential element in understanding the character of God. The New Testament reasons *both* ways: God is your Father, therefore . . . *and* You are God's children, therefore. . . .

---

21. R. B. Gaffin jr., *The Centrality of the Resurrection*, Grand Rapids, 1978, pp. 117-119.

What are the implications inherent in the idea of sonship? To paraphrase the apostle John, we may say: Look, you are the children of God, do you not realise the degree to which this shows how much God loves you (1 Jn. 3:1)? In fact John calls this love 'amazing'. It is the size and unexpectedness of it which he finds so remarkable.

By contrast we have grown somewhat accustomed to the love of God; we do not find it so very amazing. But the recognition that what we are is 'family' in relation to God, that we are his sons and daughters, and that *we* (of all people!) are his children, is calculated to produce a new and true appreciation of God as our Father. There is no higher self-image that the Christian can have, and no doctrine which will more readily help him enjoy the life of faith.

The pastoral implications of this may best be summarised by setting down, side by side, the words of the elder brother in Jesus' Parable of the Waiting Father, and the words of the apostle John. The elder brother symbolises one to whom all the privileges of God's grace have been extended, but never received. John's words express the amazed joy of one who has begun to appreciate that the gospel makes us sons and daughters of God:

Look (said the elder brother)! All these years I've been *slaving* for you (Lk. 15:29).

Look (said John)! Of what a size is the love the Father has lavished on us, that we should be called the children of God (1 Jn. 3:1).

Of these words, John Cotton, the renowned Old and New England Puritan quaintly wrote:

This reproves men's squint looking. They do not look at God's love, but at themselves and at their own corruptions and affections. It is a wonder that God's children should pore only upon their corruptions, and not consider what love it is for God to discover them and pardon them.[22]

The doctrine of sonship helps to correct our spiritual squint. It enables us to see ourselves more clearly, because it helps us to see the grace of God more clearly. The doctrine of sonship undergirds the high privileges of Christian experience.

For four decades now, William Still has faithfully expressed many elements of the biblical and reformed doctrine of the Fatherhood of God and the sonship and brotherhood of believers. I salute him with gratitude as he approaches his seventy-fifth birthday, and remind him of the promise of God to all his children:

I am the Alpha and the Omega, the Beginning and the End. To him who is thirsty I will give to drink without cost from the spring of the water of life. He who overcomes will inherit all this, *and I will be his God and he will be my son.*

Revelation 21:6.

22. John Cotton, *The First Epistle of John,*1657, ad. 3:1.

PSYCHOLOGICAL ASPECTS OF INNER HEALING

MONTAGU BARKER

In the 1970's there was a burgeoning of talking treatments, more technically known as psychotherapies or counselling programmes, directed at the elimination of emotional ills and problems from people's lives. A more recent survey quoted an American article headed "The Me Decade" describing the demand which people had for alteration of their lives. The author asked

> . . . What did they want to eliminate from their lives? Why, they took their fingers right off the old repress button and told the whole room: my husband, my wife, my homosexuality, my inability to communicate, my self hatred, self destructiveness, craven fears, puking weaknesses, primordial horrors, premature ejaculation, impotence, frigidity, subservience, laziness, alcoholism, major vices, minor vices, grim habits, twisted psyche, my tortured soul.[1]

The same survey with the title 'Let's talk about Me'[2] spoke of these therapies offering

> . . . Not merely therapy but personal growth, character transformation, psychological rebirth and even mystical experience.[3]

Immediately Christians are alerted, for words like growth, transformation and rebirth are surely the prerogative of Christian teaching and not psychological healing. The reaction of some Christians is to eschew all psychological insights and to insist on scriptural prescriptions for all emotional ails. Others however seek to reinterpret specific psychological healing approaches in Christian terms. Both approaches run into difficulties; the former by denying all the factors contributing to our personalities and by seeking miraculous healings of psychological problems or hurts, or tending to see such problems as evidence of demonic activity requiring exorcism, often with disillusionment and occasionally tragic consequences;[4] the latter by developing elaborate training schemes for psychological spiritual healing approaches which have brought disillusionment and been severely criticised even in those circles which previously espoused them.[5] But the fact remains that people *do* want to talk about themselves as never before. In our Post-Freudian era, society has become accustomed to psychological explanations of behaviour. People have an expectation of being

1. T. Wolfe, 'The 'Me' Decade', *New York Magazine*, 23 August 1976, pp. 26-40.
2. A. W. Clare, with S. Thompson, *Let's talk about me*, BBC, 1981.
3. *Idem.*, from dust jacket.
4. M. G. Barker, 'Possession and the Occult — a psychiatrist's view', *Churchman* vol. 94 no. 3, 1980, pp. 246-253.
5. D. MacIness, 'Comments on the work of Christ in the Healing of Primal Pain', *Theological Renewal* no. 7, October 1977, pp. 11-14.

offered solutions to all their problems as never before.

Christians are not immune to these influences and indeed may have an even greater expectation following the Charismatic Movement with its emphasis on change and renewal at an individual and corporate level within the church. It is not surprising that there is an explosion of Christian counselling approaches running parallel to and often in reaction to similar secular agencies. Some of the problems cited by the author of 'The Me Decade' might not be talked about so openly by Christians but the tendency to expose the deepest, most private, and guilt-producing parts of our lives and memories is being encouraged even in public albeit with safeguards in meetings for healing involving exorcisms or sessions for inner healing. It is important therefore to recognise that the present surge of interest in healings producing personal change and self actualisation is a phenomenon of contemporary Western Society and not a specifically Christian phenomenon. This is not to deny the deep spiritual hunger which may underlie this quest and which the Freudian revolution sought to rationalise but succeeded only in exposing in a new way.

There are probably in excess of 200 named counselling or therapy approaches, all claiming to heal and lead to fuller understanding and changed behaviour. In the view of one observer those counselling approaches which carry a Christian label such as healing of the memories or inner healing are not to be differentiated except in so far as they cater for the person with a religious world view as opposed to a secular world view. In fact it has been shown that there is value in this as the closer the philosophy of the healing approach is to that of the sufferer's perception of what is wrong with him, the more effective is it. Of course by the same token the secular sufferer would be helped more by a secular approach.[6]

How then are we to evaluate the approach outlined in such books as *The Experience of Inner Healing*[7] or indeed any of those experiences leading to a person claiming wholeness or integration of personality? That there is an experience which is common to many and called inner healing needs no comment. That it is a gift of God has been argued by some. That it is merely a religious variant of the contemporary search for help for hang-ups would be held by others. Accordingly let us examine the subject of Christian experience.

I would see Christian experience as the total expression of our thoughts and behaviour and awareness as Christians. This is influenced by the Holy Spirit as he speaks through the Word. This is further influenced by our theology which is our interpretation of the Christian faith and which may in turn be influenced by our own personal drives and psychological needs, in other words, our personalities. If Freud has taught us anything it is that our experience

6. J. D. Frank, *Persuason and Healing, A Comparative Study of Psychotherapy,* Revised Edition, 1973, Johns Hopkins University Press, p. 327.
7. R. C. Stapleton, *The Experience of Inner Healing,* Hodder & Stoughton, 1978.

in its broadest sense is influenced by our upbringing, by our families, by our culture and training, and I do not find that our experience as Christians is any less likely to be influenced by these factors. Indeed, to deny this would be to call in question our own Christian understanding of discipline, training and the family. These factors produce the personalities in which the Holy Spirit begins his work.

What then are the psychological factors influencing Christian experience? In other words — what makes us tick? First of all there is our genetic potential. By this I mean our inherited potential or predisposition. This is not something which is complete and immutable at conception, but our genes do contain the potential of our appearance, our intelligence and our personality, though this is constantly modified by other factors. Perhaps this is best illustrated by reference to the interaction of intellect and Christian experience. The person of lower intelligence thinks in a very concrete way. He takes an absolute approach to situations and the Christian life may appear very simple and black and white. The person of higher intelligence is more likely to be an abstract thinker and he will be concerned with the relationship of the Christian faith to philosophy, culture and business. Secondly, psychological studies have demonstrated that group and cultural pressures do influence attitudes such as honour, shame, sexuality and the expression of emotions. But the influences which are best researched are family relationships. We know that separation from the mother may produce a person with an impaired ability for stable relationships. Such an individual may have difficulty in expressing love and in receiving love in adult life. We know that when a father is absent from a home when the child is at puberty, such a child may subsequently have difficulty in sexual adjustment, with a higher incidence of sexual problems and broken relationships. We know that an experience of bereavement early in life produces an impaired ability to meet stress later in life, so that the depression could be two or three times greater in such a person than in someone who has not been bereaved. Such individuals from disturbed or broken families are more likely to show impaired relationships in later life. They will be met in church life among parsons and people alike. They are often tense, rather withdrawn, people, who protect themselves emotionally or over-depend on others. Some will fasten upon the minister as a father or husband substitute. Many will have a chronic lack of assurance, constantly trying to do better than their best. Many will take their distorted views of parenthood and fathering and project these upon God. But these are the very people who may be drawn to the warmth of a Church fellowship and although the fellowship can begin to minister to them often their approach to the Christian family is impaired and even destructive.

The impact of training on personality is too obvious to comment on at length, but people from rigid backgrounds often themselves have a rather perfectionist yet pessimistic personality. People from more relaxed backgrounds often have freer personalities but may also lack the same sense of responsibility. This is seen in Christian experience in the development of conscience. The laying down of a sense of guilt and moral values relies upon training, and so the hyper-critical and tyrannical conscience is often developed in a family of rigid behaviour and meticulous training, often with an excessive sense of guilt. Likewise our habits, those repeated regular actions of life, are instilled early on in our lives and so are difficult to break. In Christian fellowships there are those Christians who are neat, meticulous individuals, who put everything into pigeon-holes and who feel guilty if they don't have regular and set times of devotions. Others are more slap dash and unpunctual and lack order in their devotional lives, and as Christians they may not be so reliable because less disciplined. They tend not to go through the same agonies in their Christian life and devotions as the perfectionists. There is the apocryphal story of John Wesley and George Whitefield, which nevertheless illustrates this point. John Wesley was brought up in a rigid High Church household where the children were ordered by the ringing of a bell and were taught by their mother to cry silently. Whitefield was brought up in the local inn and had a much less ordered life. In adulthood, they worked together and went out on their evangelistic tours, and the story is told that they arrived one night at an inn, very tired. When they reached the room which they shared, George Whitefield threw himself on the bed exhausted while Wesley got down on his knees, opened his Bible and before setting to his devotions looked very reproachfully at George Whitefield and said 'George, George, is this your Calvinism?' At 2am in the morning George woke up and found John still on his knees, fast asleep over his Bible, so he shook him and said 'John, John, is this your Arminianism?' It was not their differing theological systems, but their family backgrounds which led them in their fatigue to react with completely different attitudes to devotions. So often this sort of reaction does depend not upon our theology but upon something within our backgrounds and personalities.

Personality, then is very much the product of all these factors working together in a complex and dynamic way and we must remember that the Holy Spirit works within our God-given potential. He has to begin with us as we are, with our backgrounds and our problems. He may have a lot of very basic personality remaking to do and even if we do not recognise this our friends and relatives will. So when the Holy Spirit works in our lives, He works within the individuality of our personalities and it is this which accounts for the rich variety of Christian biography. We have the remote and logical Calvin; the warm tempestuous Luther; the fastidious and over-organised John Wesley; and the freer more liberated Whitefield, son of a publican. God used each greatly and in different ways and who would dare to rank them spiritually? Theologically they stand in absolute agreement regarding Christ and pardon from sins but their experience of God's dealing with them personally was different. In particular their doctrinal systems widely differed and unhappily their followers were often bitter enemies. Whatever may be the true understanding regarding the Biblical passages disagreed upon, the problem in terms of division and hostility seemed so often to occur in this area of personality and experience.

Let me take this further by mentioning some phrases which have been used over the past 300 years within evangelicalism: 'Conversion experience', 'Sense of assurance', 'Entire sanctification', 'Experience of the fullness of the Holy Spirit', 'Experience of the baptism of the Spirit', 'The experience of brokenness', 'The experience of tongues', 'Sinless perfection', 'Charismatic movement', to which may be added 'The experience of inner healing', all these phrases have been associated with division and conflict within the church. All these phrases contain Biblical words but it is the use of the extra words 'experience of', 'movement', 'sinless', 'entire', 'higher', which has produced division among Christians and caused the opposing ranks to line up against each other. As we look at the history of these phrases, each one has arisen out of the deep dissatisfaction of groups of Christians as they have viewed the apparent poverty of their experience as Christians compared with what they believed as Christians. In most instances their quest was followed by an experience associated with a new joy in believing and devotion to Christ and a new love for their fellow Christians. But in each case they followed a desire to systematise their experience, then to reproduce it. In some there followed a third stage. Not only did they seek to reproduce the circumstances of their experience, but they sought refuge in their common experience and used the experience as a means of identifying each other, and as a token of entry to closer fellowship. So that whatever truth was there, it became obscured by party strife and division.

Let me take one particular experience; the experience of conversion. We are familiar with it and value it, but conversion is not one of the main Biblical themes. There is no theology worked out by theologians and there is little emphasis in New Testament preaching on conversion. The real Biblical terms are repentance, new birth, justification. Augustine much preferred the word 'change' to conversion. Luther preferred the word 'repentance'. He mentioned conversion in his whole collected works four times only and he looked upon conversion as not a single act but as something repeated through life. When speaking of conversion, Calvin spoke of it as 'Being converted to God gradually and by sure degrees of repentance' and he acknowledged that this began when we first turned to God.[8] Conversion generally in the course of time became equated with regeneration in the minds of many but occurred with or without a

8. T. H. L. Parker, in article 'Conversion', *A Dictionary of Christian Theology*, ed. A. Richardson, SCM, London, 1969.

conscious experience and was due to the work of the Holy Spirit in our lives and witnessed to by the fruit of the Spirit.

It was not until the seventeenth century that the experience of conversion became a controversial issue. At that time the church was filled with many who were doctrinally correct but without any indication of spiritual life. The German pietists in their spiritual struggling and agonisings had a sudden experience of active commitment and this became associated with an experience of assurance of divine grace. Somewhat later the Moravian Brethren had the same assurance but they had gone through no strugglings. They had only the immediate joyful apprehension of a loving Father, so much so that the pietists doubted the reality of the conversion of Count Zinzendorf the Moravian Leader. Each party sought to stereotype its experience of conversion and assurance and then use this as the test of new birth. It is partly from this background that modern evangelicalism is descended, and there are still churches where a certain kind of conversion experience is expected, and even demanded, and by a process of suggestion and exclusion the pattern tends to be repeated. The more suggestible the individual the more readily will the experience be reproduced. The less suggestible the individual, the greater may be the difficulty in reproducing the expected experience and consequently the greater the distress for that individual. This was particularly noteworthy in the Kentucky Camp Meetings of the nineteenth century in the United States. Whole families with adolescent children were marched off to these yearly meetings, and then in response to a week's preaching all the children returned soundly converted every year. That was the way it was done. This is still seen in some denominations in Europe, where sudden conversion experiences are particularly valued.

There was a questionnaire on conversion given to some theological students some years ago. Among the students of a particular Baptist College, ninety seven per cent of the students had had a conversion experience. The majority of them had had a sudden conversion experience. Within the evangelical Anglican College studied, ninety three per cent of the students had had a conversion experience but only fifty per cent of them had had a sudden conversion experience. Within an Anglo-Catholic College fifty per cent of the students had had a conversion experience but none of them had had a sudden conversion experience. Even among evangelicals with the same theology of regeneration the frequency of the actual type of conversion experience may be very different according to church background.

The suddenness of our experience of conversion may be an accident of our backgrounds and personalities, but the fact that the Holy Spirit is working in our lives is not. It is not the *experience* of conversion but the *fact* that we have turned and continued to turn to Christ which is truly the sign of the Holy Spirit working in our lives.

In Christ we become new men and new women. As Christians we have new models in our relationships. We have a new power and a new teacher in the Holy Spirit, with a new hope in the resurrection of the body. But we still have our old genes, we still have our old family backgrounds and even the best of families are still affected by the fall. Accordingly all the problems from our families and all that has gone into making us has to be retrained, retaught, and redirected. But we do not have to cling to our old models of behaviour. We do not have to obey the impulses to behave in the way which we previously accepted. We do not have to act out our instinctual drives. There is a new law there, a new model and a new power and in this sense we are free from the law of sin and death.[9] We are not obliged to reproduce experiences. God has given us his word, he has surrounded us by his people and in them he has given us new models.[10] But we must begin where we are.

In Romans chapter 8 we read that all creation is subjected to futility, in bondage to decay and groaning in travail and not just creation but ourselves. We along with creation wait with eager longing for the glory that is to be revealed.[11] And the work of all who minister and pastor is to prepare men and women for that day. But there is a tension between what we are and what we hope to be. There is a tension between what we preach and what we accept within the fellowship. There is a tension between what we show to others and what we do in ourselves. The people of God and the Christian world have always known this tension, as did Paul. The Roman Catholic church made two standards — that of the religious life for those specially determined and the secular life for the rest. Protestantism has tended to deal with the tension by producing recurrent perfectionist sects with their ever more defined experiences, constantly seeking for an ever clearer and indisputable evidence of regeneration. Paul describes what we now experience in Romans chapter 7. He describes what we shall experience in Romans chapter 8 and I suppose we could say that in Romans chapter 12 to 16 he speaks of how we act and behave in the meantime. There is no doctrine of 'experience' in the Bible. There is a revelation of God, Father, Son and Holy Spirit whose presence and power in our lives we may experience in a host of ways. The actual experience of Christians does not normally cause division until that experience is made normative for others and is given a special significance or used as a proof of a special relationship with God. The test of the presence of God the Holy Spirit in our lives is the presence of the fruit of the Spirit. Luther once prayed: 'God give us the experience of being freed from experience.' He saw himself how experience is a dangerous mentor and guide. One Scottish theologian of a hundred years ago said:

There are innumerable moulds in God's world. Why do we coop up God's

9. Rom. 7:13-25.
10. 1 Thess. 1:6-7.
11. Rom. 8:22-23.

grace in narrow man-made channels, and say this is the way God has worked and will work? His greatness is no-ways displayed more illustriously than in the spreading out of His gifts in a thousand different ways. There is a manifoldness in His operation that surely proclaims the beauty of His holiness.[12]

It is from this perspective that we should look at some of the contemporary approaches to healing within the Charismatic Movement, notably the experience of Inner Healing referred to earlier. This is an approach to healing which leans heavily upon modern psychological theories and practices.

There are of course great difficulties in biblical terminology and interpretation as soon as we begin to speak of 'Healing' today. In some writings salvation and healing seem to be used almost synonymously. However exponents of Inner Healing define the term as a 'Healing of the soul . . . a healing at both the spiritual and the emotional levels'.[13] There are those whose backgrounds and family experiences appear to be so devoid of love and caring that they can recall only a rejection and inconsistency from their parents. Accordingly they feel they cannot break through the blank despair of never experiencing joy and peace and would therefore attribute lack of assurance and growth in the Christian faith as well as their lack of joy and peace in the Lord as being due to these earlier experiences. It is to the needs of these individuals apparently stunted and retarded in their emotional and therefore their spiritual development that the practitioners of Inner Healing have offered particular help and to whom they have turned their special attention.

The argument goes as follows. These people require Inner Healing, that is healing of the mind, will, heart and emotions as something apart from physical healing.[14] Just as the Lord healed when he was on earth so can he heal today and not just our bodies but all the emotional scars of broken hurtful or absent relationships in the past. As Christ comes in salvation so does he come in healing of the deepest and inmost parts of our being. Christ can be brought into the most hurtful and murkiest parts of our pasts with transforming power bringing 'release', 'new transparency' and a 'real knowing that God loves you'.[15] Such writers as Father Scanlon outline the approaches and techniques which can be acquired in achieving this. He claims:

> We have prayed for women who hated men, men who rebelled against all authority that figures in their life, men and women who are convinced they were unlovable and acted that way, men and women who wouldn't place trust in anyone else, alcoholics, dope addicts, schizophrenics, those whose lives were substantially impaired by fears of darkness, being alone, failure, sex, and most commonly those with dominating feelings of guilt

12. W. Knight, ed., *Colloquia Peripatetica, Conversations with Rabbi Duncan,* Oliphant, 1907, p 111.
13. R. Faricy, *Praying for Inner Healing,* SCM, 1979, p. 5.
14. M. Scanlan, *Inner Healing,* Veritas Publications, 1977, p. 9.
15. *Idem.,* pp. 55-61.

and inferiority. In every case where there was a series of contacts there has been improvement. In each category mentioned there has been a person substantially or fully healed as best we can determine.[16]

Ruth Carter Stapleton in one of her books heads a chapter 'There is a solution to every problem'.[17]

However, words of caution must be placed alongside these claims. The emphasis upon the sacrament of penance and its equation with the sacrament of spiritual healing is striking in the writings of Roman Catholic practitioners. The Jesuit theologian Robert Faricy links inner healing with the sacraments of penance and anointing of the sick and claims that inner healing is the renewal of these sacraments.[18] It is difficult not to feel that these specific probings and guidings associated with the process of being led through the stages of inner healing by the healer are derived from the techniques of the confessional and have a similar psychological ritual.[19] Such an approach is alien to those from a Protestant tradition but the same dissection of past experience and behaviour with its steps to healing are to be found in Mrs Stapleton's books.[20] However while ritual can be valuable in helping us incorporate truths into minds and behaviour the very practice of rituals is well known to produce subjective release in anxiety and tension in situations with no spiritual dimension.

Furthermore the fact that a person recalls 'memories' does not give authenticity to those 'memories'. If a healer uses or has a particular interest in memories within his healing methods then the sufferer will tend to produce memories as part of the transaction between healer and sufferer. Our generation has been conditioned by fifty years of psychoanalytic doctrine into accepting the necessity for uncovering repressed memories as the root causes of behavioural and emotional difficulties. The uncovering of and gaining of insight into these memories does not necessarily change things and this has led to disillusionment and a wide spread movement within the so called modern psychotherapies of fantasyzing round these memories or acting them out in some form as a way of gaining emotional release and relief. The process of inner healing involves the fantasyzing of Christ within the old painful memories as a way of introducing him into those areas which have caused pain and unwanted behaviour. It is claimed that the taking of Christ back into those memories in imagination releases, cleanses and renews the old situations. This is very much like a technique whereby the current problem is put into a 'memory' which is then replaced by a good or neo-memory. Indeed this so called guided imagery technique is taught and used in some of the humanistic psychotherapies as a way of exposing hidden emotions. The exposure

---

16. *Idem.*, pp. 12-13.
17. R. C. Stapleton, *The Gift of Inner Healing*, Hodder, 1976, p. 101.
18. R. Faricy, *op. cit.*, p. 5.
19. R. Faricy, *ibid.*, pp. 13-14.
20. R. C. Stapleton, *The Experience of Inner Healing*, pp. 162-167.

25

and expression of emotions in this way is not without its dangers.[21] Nor does it mean that the associated fantasies are factual. For example the person who had no father does not become as though he had a father by imagining Jesus in all the fatherless situations of the past. He may of course be released from the bitterness of not having had a father in the past in order to be open to receive lots of different father type experiences within the fellowship in the present.

Indeed suggestion either by the healer or group probably plays a large part in the recorded experiences in such situations. While on a visit to the United States I forced myself to watch 'an hour of real live miracles' on television. As the Pentecostalist healer touched each individual on the forehead when declaring healing so did each afflicted individual fall back senseless into the arms of waiting attendants only to rise 'healed' in a few seconds. In a credo programme on ITV on exorcism in December 1980 I was intrigued to see the identical ritual and associated phenomenon during the exorcism of demons occurring in a Full Gospel Businessman's Meeting in Bristol. This group has of course strong links with American Pentecostalism. By contrast in the two House Churches (150 miles apart) visited and filmed for the programme the exorcism of the demons was accompanied by a reported experience of coughing or vomiting up of the unclean spirits. The Anglican exorcism filmed was done by a priest in full canonicals at the altar rail and was accompanied only by shudders and jerkings. The cynic may be tempted to reflect on how accommodating of Satan to behave true to form for each denomination.

The production of certain experiences and phenomena, no matter how worthy, are not in themselves evidence of the work of the Holy Spirit and using similar techniques, secular and Christian groups can produce apparently identical experiences although understood and attributed quite differently. Let me illustrate this by taking excerpts from accounts of eighteenth century Methodist groups and comparing them with similar accounts from twentieth century humanistic psychological groups. The eighteenth century Methodist states: 'My design was . . . to have a select company to whom I might unbosom myself on all occasions without reserve. The humanist group leader states: 'A climate of mutual trust develops out of this mutual freedom to express real feelings positive and negative.' Again the early methodist states: 'They begin to bear one another's burdens and naturally to care for one another.' The contemporary humanist states: 'People begin caring for each other and supporting each other.' Again the early Christian fellowship is described in these terms:

> When a happy correspondence between the outward walk and inward piety of believers is discovered, which can be known only by the disclosure of the interior life, we are not only prepared to comfort encourage and

21. G. Stanley, Do you know what T-groups are?, *Christian Graduate* vol. 27 no. 4, December 1974, pp. 108-111.

strengthen one another, but form an intimacy of the holiest nature a union of the strongest character.

The contemporary humanist group leader states:

> Participants feel a closeness and intimacy which they have not felt even with their spouses or members of their own family, because they have revealed themselves here more deeply.

Let us give the last word to the participants of a twentieth century sensitivity group where the

> Participants almost unanimously speak of marathons, immediately afterward and for years afterward as a worthwhile and moving experience, the words, 'I felt reborn' are often uttered.[22]

The danger is in thinking that because we are in a distinctive Christian tradition the phenomena are of necessity of the Spirit of God and we are therefore safe from contemporary secularism. The facts are that ingredients are common to all 'healing situations' whether organic or psychological, pagan or Christian, as a result of which the sufferer has a greater chance of *feeling* better, even cured. This has been well researched and persuasively presented by Professor J. S. Frank:

> The most reasonable assumption is that all forms of psychotherapy that persist must do some good. Furthermore it is likely that the lack of clear differences in the improvement rate from different forms of psychotherapy result from features common to them all.[23]

Professor Frank goes on to describe these features which he has arrived at as a result of painstaking and careful research. First of all he speaks of the quality of the relationship between sufferer and healer which should include a confidence in the healer and a communication that he cares and accepts the sufferer in spite of all that he is or has done. Secondly, there should be a designated place where the healing can take place that is a place set apart from the rest of life where the sufferer can suspend his critical faculties and feel that he will not be held accountable in daily life for whatever he says and does at this time. Thirdly, there must be an acceptable rationale for the healing procedure which is shared by healer and sufferer alike. And concordance of opinion regarding the nature of the problem is essential for the fourth ingredient of healing to take place. This is the necessity for a special ritual or procedure to be followed. There must be something which the sufferer can do under the guidance of the healer. Whether it is taking pills from the doctor, receiving penances from the Priest or submitting to techniques of a Counsellor does not greatly matter for more than fifty per cent of the experience of relief and healing will come from the expectation that the ritual itself will be effective.[24] Mere anecdotal accounts of special healings however

---

22. T. C. Oden, 'The Intensive-Group Experience' in *The New Pietism*, Westminster Press, 1972.
23. J. D. Frank, *idem.*, p. 22.
24. J. D. Frank, *et al.*, *Effective Ingredients of Successful Psychotherapy*, Brunner/Mazel, 1978, p. 31.

impressive the evidence may be to us individually prove nothing except Frank's thesis. This in no way discounts the relief a person may feel after such interventions as Inner Healing but only true controls and careful recorded follow-ups such as are to be found in medical clinical trials can show whether there is an extra dimension in such approaches as Inner Healing. Even then, neither the relief of the person nor any clinical trial can provide proof of a specific spiritual dimension.[25]

The giving of a theological framework to a technique or ritual does not necessarily indicate that that ritual is a vehicle for use by the Holy Spirit. Indeed the more we resort to techniques the more likely we are to imprison the individual psychologically and reproduce psychological stereotypes masquerading as Christian experience. This is amply witnessed to by the effects of certain types of high pressure evangelism in the past. Furthermore as in many of the contemporary healing movements, Christian and humanist, there is a tendency to dualism which is not Biblical. Human suffering is seen as either organic or spiritual and the place of physical methods of treatment is often rejected or not recognised in those people who are mentally ill and ought to be treated with anti-depressants or electro-convulsive therapy. There is ample research to show the value and necessity for physical treatments in certain well defined conditions and the total disregard of this area of treatment can be mischievous and to some extent reflects the distrust of 'drugs' and 'ECT' in some sections of the contemporary 'Your healing is within you' scene. By contrast there is an apparent complete acceptance of the theories of the depth psychologies with their insistence on repressed memories hurts and emotions as the cause and location of our hang-ups and non-ability to do what we want, shown in phrases like,

> Bill had become a victim of childhood circumstances . . . he was not personally responsible for the circumstances which *made* him respond in the way he did . . . his parents were responsible through their inability to show him real affection.

This has the mechanistic quality of the philosophy of the total behaviourist. Even Mrs Stapleton confidently and uncritically accepts in her case history of a homosexual that 'It was obvious why men interested him — viz the death of his father when he was eight'.[26] This particular theory is not proven and at best can be only a partial explanation.

Clearly to feel good is not wrong. Nor can it be wrong to use such techniques of healing (as outlined by Professor Frank) which help us feel better. But it is *being* good which is the mark of the Christian growing up into spiritual maturity. The mature Christian is someone who has his faculties trained by practice to distinguish good from evil (Hebrews 5:14) and is showing work and love in serving his fellow

25. T. Martin, *Kingdom Healing*, Marshalls, 1981, p. 95.
26. R. C. Stapleton, *The Gift of Inner Healing*, p. 105.

Christians (Hebrews 6:1). When the Apostle John is answering the question as to how we may know that we have passed from death to life, he does not point to an experience but to tests of our attitude to Christ, our love for our fellow Christians and changes in our daily behaviour. Psychological release may help us here, but there is a goal beyond that for the Christian.

'Self authentication' and 'being free to be myself' may be worthwhile in enabling openness and honesty in relationships instead of a guilty servitude, and that can only be good. Nevertheless the Christian looks beyond that. He seeks an honest appraisal of himself (Romans 12:3) and is encouraged to stir up his fellow Christians (Hebrews 10:24-25) but its purpose is the producing of good works not just good feelings. Whatever feelings we may have, it is being good and doing good works which show the work of the Holy Spirit in our lives and which distinguish between that which is part of our human interaction and that which is the result of God, Father, Son and Holy Spirit active in our lives within the fellowship.

I am sure that if challenged those who practice Inner Healing would deny that this is a complete approach to pastoral caring. But there is a danger in an approach so attractive in what it seems to offer that it may supplant and detract from the place of preaching the word within the fellowship. It may be significant that Inner Healing approaches were developed in the context of the Charismatic Renewal within denominations which had no strong tradition of expository preaching but had a more sacramental tradition.[27] This is a general theme which I have discussed elsewhere[28] but as William Still has written:

> The pastor is the shepherd of the flock and feeds the flock upon God's Word and therefore the bulk of pastoral work is done through the ministry of the Word. Only the residue of problems and difficulties which remain following the ministry of the Word require to be dealt with in private.[29]

There is however an attractiveness in the Inner Healing approach in that here there is an attempt to think theologically and psychologically in approaching emotional suffering. While it may be fair to say that those who popularise Inner Healing seem to pay scant regard to the fact that our faulted genes and imperfect family relationships are still *facts* till we die and no amount of Inner Healing will remove those facts, yet the emphasis that Christ's salvation reaches into our past is surely Biblical. Christ has entered into our humanity, all of it, (Hebrews 2:14-18) therefore we are not wholly bound by our past and while it may still affect us we are no longer paralysed by it — but can with confidence find mercy and find grace to help in time of need (Hebrews 4:15-16). To fantasize with Christ has a suggestion of self deceit and of non reality for the 'New memories' are still only fantasies,

27. T. Martin, *op. cit.*, p. 76.
28. M. G. Barker, 'Biblical and Psychological Methods of Pastoral Care', in *Behavioural Sciences: A Christian Perspective*, ed. Malcolm Jeeves, IVP, 1984, pp. 230-245.
29. W. Still, *More about the Work of the Pastor*, Didasko Press, Preface.

yet the emphasis that we can deliberately and consciously replace evil and destructive thoughts with good and wholesome thoughts is surely Biblical. We are instructed to 'Put on Christ' (Galatians 3:27) and *think* about those things which are honourable, just, pure and lovely (Philippians 4:5-9).

Here is an attempt then to apply Christian teaching to the places where men and women with all their struggles and failings hurt and long for help, but so often feel that they have to go to the psychotherapy market place for aid. Here is an attempt to understand and apply the Word of God within our relationships where the minister is himself a 'vulnerable equal'.[30] How little preaching even expository preaching, has such a quality of immediacy and application. How few pastors are themselves members of the body and open to pastoring. There are many features of the 'Experience of Inner Healing' which should be regarded with caution like all the other special experiences instanced throughout the Christian centuries. But the fact that they recur regularly dressed up in the garb of contemporary movements surely indicates a longing of men and women to know a quality of preaching and Christian fellowship which affects our whole being and sends us out to serve the Lord in joyful service.

30. R. C. Stapleton, *The Experience of Inner Healing,* p. 201.

THE LAND IS MINE...AND YOU ARE...MY TENANTS*:

reflections on the Biblical view of Man and Nature

ROWLAND MOSS

The story of man in society as it is unfolded in Scripture begins in a garden and is consummated in a city (Gen.1:28-31; 2:8-17; Rev.21:9-22:5). Between its birth in abundant provision and delegated responsibility and its completion in the blessed felicity of the continual presence and superabundant mercies of God the Lord, the story moves through many phases and dispensations, in the manner of the unfolding of an epic drama, or of the development and coherent growth of a grand symphony. At every point the changing patterns are rooted in the relation of man to the natural world, in both its inanimate and its non-human animate dimensions, for the Lord God is the creator of heaven and earth and everything that is in them. This relationship of man to the natural world is a constant theme throughout Scripture, but one which is perhaps rarely surveyed as a whole, though particular facets are more frequently examined.

Two sermons preached by William Still in Gilcomston South Church on such topics are deeply embedded in the memory, and epitomise two themes which form essential motifs in the inspired structure of this supreme symphony of God's sovereign grace and incomprehensible glory. One was an exposition of Leviticus chapter 25, which emphasised the fact that the earth and its abundant provisions for the needs of man belong to God, and that God requires responsible use and active gratitude as conditions for the fulness of blessing in that provision. The other, an exposition of Psalm 104, saw the wonder of the created universe as an expression of the unfathomable wisdom of God, as an object of God's pleasure, and as a vehicle for his praise. Both utterances were not only inspiring, but also pointedly salutary, for an aspiring natural scientist in the early days of his career in agricultural research in tropical Africa. In this essay these and other themes dealing with man in relation to nature will be explored by ranging throughout Scripture. Such an approach must of necessity mean that many profound issues must be left unexplored, and some points of controversy remain undiscussed. It is my hope that the broad conspectus may provide a framework into which more particular questions may be fitted, and suggest links which may illuminate more specific issues.

The symphonic analogy may be utilised further. The thematic

*(Leviticus) 25:23 (NIV))

approach suggests a treatment in sonata form. The main themes are all stated in the early chapters of Genesis, forming the primary *exposition*; they are traced and developed in the history of the covenant people under the old dispensation, in the events of that story, and the religion and literature associated with those events — a *development* section. This grows to the point when the *re-capitulation* can be postponed no longer, and all things are summed up in Christ Jesus (Col.1:15-20); from that a further *development* leads to a glorious climactic *coda*, in which the choirs of saints and angels, the trumpets of judgment, the harps of sweet rejoicing and contentment, articulate the spontaneous and unfettered praise of a new heavens and a new earth redeemed, transmuted and glorified out of the shattered and divided futility of the old. The symphony begins with the glory of the old creation and ends with the greater glory of the new creation, of which Christ Jesus is the first fruit, and in which we who belong to him are already a part. And all to the glory of God the Lord, who is above all and through all and in all.

Exposition

The book of Scripture begins with two complementary narratives concerned with the relation of the transcendent God to the book of nature. The early chapters of the Bible are carefully constructed documents displaying an intricacy of designed style that marks them out as quite unique in the literature of the ancient world, and perhaps of any age. The symmetry of their arrangement from their overall grouping of material to their use of particular words and combinations of words and the significant images by which the events recorded are described marks them out as uniquely inspired in both the divine and the literary sense. Nor can their extreme age be any longer seriously doubted. It can be no surprise that the Holy Spirit inspired the ancient author to such heights of literary skill when the importance of the truth to be conveyed is appreciated.

The craft in the use of language matches the sublime content of the themes. The world and the universe in which man lives, in all its intricate complexity and inconceivable extent, its awesome power and inexpressible beauty, is entirely and completely the product of the Word of God; *God speaks* — and *it is*! (Gen.1:3,6,9,14,20,24,26). Moreover, he takes pleasure in his work, for he sees that it is good, indeed very good (Gen.1:4,10,12,18,21,25,31). But more. Man is not simply part of that creation, full of wonder and glory as it is, for *God speaks to him* and he with God (Gen.1:28-30; 2:16-17; 3:9-13), and with such intimacy that God's presence can be known in the garden as really as that of another human being (Gen.3:8). Nor, though his communion with God is ultimate and all-sufficient, does he remain solitary, for God creates a complementary being of equal abilities and comparable status before God to be a 'helpmeet' for him (Gen.1:27;

2:18-24). Moreover the purpose of that complementary person is that together they may produce a race of similar individuals to live together in the wonder of the wider creation (Gen.1:28; 2:24).

This is the grand triumphant major key theme of the symphony of nature — a created and sustained world of abundant provision, exquisite delight, supreme beauty, and all to be enjoyed in social intercourse through communion with God the Lord. Indeed it is a world in which God himself takes supreme delight. It is not thereby a world of effortless self-satisfaction and indolent pleasure; the theme includes a motif which involves effort and responsibility. God sets apart a garden in the midst of his creation, a region provided with all that was necessary for a satisfying life, but man is set within it to cultivate it and to care for it. Man is charged with responsibility as the steward of God's creation, to make it productive, and to tend and preserve it for God's pleasure and glory, and thus for his own blessing (Gen.2:8-17). To test the freedom of man's obedience in this role, his stewardship is fenced with one, and one only, prohibition, and also by one positive and precise implied requirement; he is *not* to eat the fruit of the tree of the knowledge of good and evil, but he *needs* to eat the fruit of the tree of life (cf. Gen.2:16-17 with Gen.2:9).

The second subject introduces a dark minor key. The flowing beauty of the first subject is abruptly interrupted by the introduction of the sharp discord of a dissonant element in the harmony. An unresolved discordant clash jars the ear: "*Has* God said you shall not...?" (Gen.3:1). This subtle suggestion from the implacable rebel against the order and rule and utter supremacy of God insinuates itself into the pattern, and quickly becomes the dominant element, as man disobeys the direct command, denies his dependence on God, and refuses to accept the very contingent nature of the created order. He arrogates to himself the right to act without the constraint of outside standards, he seizes the bountiful gifts of God as though they were his own, and he proudly asserts that the created order is the only reality worth considering. And man has been doing the same ever since.

God's judgment is swift, clear, and absolutely appropriate. Disobedience brings retribution, independence produces alienation, and the making absolute of that which is relative and contingent divorces it from the very source of its balance and cohesion (Gen.3:14-21). In one act the basis of morality is flouted, the foundation of social harmony cracked, and the fundamental balance of the whole created order shaken to its roots. All that was once in gracious and serene communion with man now becomes implacably against him — God the Lord, his fellow man, nature and the universe itself. The fruitful and constructive co-operation of life in the garden under the loving and joyful control of God the Lord becomes a constant labour to wrest from nature the necessitites for mere animal life, a continual effort to maintain social cohesion and minimise the inevitable conflict, and there is no longer any claim on God's help and assistance (Gen.3:22-24).

Nevertheless, embedded almost unnoticed in the dark tones of the jagged, grating, dissonant second subject, are a few notes which as a motif are destined to grow and develop so as to dominate the development as it unfolds to its glorious climax. It is subtly interwoven and integrated with the first subject so that at the great climax they are one in their transformation. For the second subject is there set aside, or rather revealed for what it really is and purged and purified by that insignificant motif, so that the glory of creation is magnified by the glory of final judgment and the supreme glory of costly redemption. Thus is produced a new creation whose wonder and beauty and purity transcends by orders of magnitude that of the first creation, which God himself even then pronounced very good. This motif is the promise that the offspring of the woman will crush the head of the root of all evil, symbolised by the serpent (Gen.3:15b). The apostle Paul, at the resolution of the climax, recalls this quite specifically when he writes to the Christians at Rome: "The God of peace will soon crush Satan under your feet." (Rom.16:20). The motif in Genesis, though clearly referring pre-eminently to Christ on whom the whole symphony centres, is also a promise to all who participate in the redemption he buys by his once-for-all sacrifice of himself. The apostle to the Gentiles also makes clear in the same letter that the blood-bought redemption is an act and a process which includes the whole of the created universe by virtue of its relationship to man in the creative and redemptive purpose of God (Rom.8:18-25).

Thus the main themes are stated and linked, and the basic elements in their development are hinted at subtly but none-the-less suggestively. But the symphony is not simply the product of human creativity, however divinely inspired; it is not a human attempt to express in invented stories, however wonderful, the facts of the human predicament as they are experienced by all men at all times. The symphony concerns actual real events in the world in which man in fact lives; God is composing the symphony by working out his purpose through the events of the history of the universe and earth and man, though as they are narrated by the writer the Holy Spirit uses figurative devices to bring out their meaning. These themes are of vital concern to all men in all ages and in all places: a fallen creature trying to be what he is not; a fallen world of nature disrupted in its working and groaning in the futility of its emasculated glory; and human societies wracked by tension and torn by the conflict which inevitably follows from moving the centre of all existence from God the Lord to his appointed steward. The tenant makes himself the owner as well as the occupier. And the form of the life within which all men have subsequently worked out their individual and collective destinies is thus closely defined. Man is free to defy God and sin, but only within the prescribed framework for disobedience. The true freedom of responsibility to a loving and caring God is exchanged for the bondage of self-seeking and obedience to another master whose attributes are the antithesis of all that is good and pure and holy and beautiful. The thrice-blessed tenant becomes the thrice-cursed slave — apart from the sheer grace of God in redemption.

Development

The development begins with the promised pain of childbirth (Gen.4:1-2), the toil of working the soil and tending the flocks (v2; & 7:29), and the tension within the family, leading to fratricide (4:3-8). But, though God the Lord is no longer accessible and available, he is still very much present, in both mercy and judgment. And at the outset the fundamental division of the human race is established, into those who turn to God and say, "Thy will be done", and those *to whom* He says, ultimately and reluctantly, "your will be done", as C. S. Lewis so aptly puts it. Abel and Cain are universal types. So mankind multiplies in numbers, but not in wisdom and devotion. Man devises, no doubt through the common grace of God, new technologies of using God's earth, and of expressing the creativity not lost, though grossly corrupted, through the fall (Gen.4:17,20-22). But, despite the deep yearning after God (4:26), degeneration into rebellion and gross immorality increasingly infects the whole race, until an act of universal judgment becomes inevitable (Gen.6:11-13). The very natural creation which God had provided for man's pleasure, profit, and provision becomes, paradoxically, the instrument of that judgment (Gen.7:11-12). But then sin is a paradox; the declaration of independence by the tenant turns the very property of his lease against him. The confusion of freedom with anarchy produces bondage, and a bondage which extends to nature from man. Early in the symphony it is the second subject which is dominant. Both Cain and Abel bring to God an offering which is the fruit of their labour in using God's earth to meet their ordinary needs. But Abel's offering is a vicarious offering of himself, a demonstration of his recognition of his need of redemption. Thus nature becomes a symbol of the need and the means of redemption. So with Noah and the flood; as natural forces are the medium for judgment, so their right use in obedience to God the Lord becomes the means and the type of salvation. Noah builds an ark which uses the laws of flotation as a means of preservation through judgment; more than that, it is the way of salvation for *both* the chosen of God and of animal nature (Gen.6:17-22; 7:1-4; cf. 1 Pet.3:18-22). No sooner has God the Lord renewed his covenant with man in nature (sealed by a visible sign which is itself a natural phenomenon produced by the transmutation of light, the symbol of the righteousness of God, through the instrument of judgment, the retreating stormclouds), when Noah plants a vineyard, abuses its products, and falls into gross sin. But yet again the hint of the redemptive theme is there, for Shem and Japheth, realising the deep moral significance of their father's recumbent nakedness, chastely cover the unseemly sight of the sinful stupor of the man who had so recently experienced the glorious deliverance by the sovereign grace of God (Gen.9:8-23). This renewed covenant is, significantly, a covenant between God the Lord and all mankind in Noah, and *all living creatures* (9:9-11;16). It is an *everlasting* covenant; God is committed by his promise never again to destroy life on earth by water: perhaps here in the earliest passages of the symphony there is also the implicit promise of redemption and renewal, a nuance of the new heavens and the new earth which are yet to be.

The second subject is transformed into a new dimension when man uses his technological creativity in transforming the mineral resources of the earth into the blasphemous construction at Babel (Gen.11:1-9). God's judgment is then to inhibit the communication of ideas by confusing language, which is not only the facilitator of creative thought, but also the very stuff of social and cultural cohesion. And in all problems of human conflict and disagreement there is always an essential element of non-communication, an inablility fully to appreciate the real content of the opposing point of view. The confusion not only inhibits the transfer of wrong ideas,.but also of good and true notions. In the very judgment therefore is implicit the necessity of the direct work of God if truth is to prevail and right understanding to spread. The word of God applied by the Holy Spirit is thus the pre-requisite for effectuation of redemption.

The theme of redemption then begins to become increasingly prominent. Shem and his descendants are chosen by God as the vehicle for his special revelation of himself. And Abraham is called out to be the progenitor of the nation to whom God commits that revelation and its concomitant responsibility, to be the father of that spiritual Israel which is the company of all faithful people in all ages and in every place, and to be the recipient of the first concrete articulation of that covenant of grace which is the only basis of redemption of both man and nature (Gen.12:1-9; 13:14-17; 15:1-21; 17:17-22). In that covenant God the Lord not only promises unique offspring, but also, and equally, a *land* — a specific area of the earth's surface to provide for the needs of his holy people. The parallel with the promise and provision of God to Adam in the garden can scarcely be missed.

Throughout the old dispensation of the covenant of grace the intimate connection of the observance of their obligations and the ability of the land to provide for the needs of the people is a constantly recurring theme. The chosen people are tenants in their new God-given land flowing with milk and honey, and they are to behave as befits tenants. Abraham and the other patriarchs never settled in the land, though they attained their final resting place there, for first the people of God had themselves to multiply and be subjected to cruel bondage (Ex.1:6-7; 11-14; 20-22). Surely during the sojourn in Egypt the people of Israel must have seen and discerned both the benefits and the temptations of a sedentary life in which needs are richly met from the bountiful earth, for ancient Egypt was a richly fertile land. As the poor they suffered oppression by the rich; as slaves they endured the pain of providing treasure cities to safeguard the ill-gotten gains of a ruling dynasty; as servants of Yahweh, the Creator Lord of heaven and earth, they saw the results of the worship of false gods and the deification of man. Surely they were well warned of the insidious web of evil which could be woven by God's enemy, if man treated the riches of God's earth as his own, an all too potent temptation in a sedentary culture richly provided with the means of subsistence.

Under Moses, by the miraculous deliverance from bondage in Egypt, the twelve tribes are constituted a people, and the trek to Sinai brings them face-to-face with the awesome presence of Yahweh, and they learn that salvation and deliverance imply significant, indeed all-embracing responsibilities. The response to the boundless grace of God includes direct reference to nature. The fourth commandment requires rest for animals as well as man; the tenth forbids covetousness with reference to the animals, and by implication, the land of another. The tablets of this law are given with a terrifying display of the majestic magnificence of natural forces, and Yahweh is there within them. Thus at Sinai the themes of nature belonging to God and existing in its own right to glorify him, and that of the responsible use of the resources of nature by man, come together, echoing the exposition of Genesis 1 and 2 (Ex.19:16 - 20:21).

The detailed instructions contained in later chapters of Exodus, in Leviticus, and in the Deuteronomic parallels, display no less a concern for the right use of nature, and its intrinsic value to God. Non-human nature is to be treated with consideration, even compassion. And in the laws of hygiene may be seen the redemptive activity of God as in some measure mitigating the results of the curse of Genesis 3. It is in the laws of tithing and of the sabbath, however, that the elements of responsible use and the inherent value of nature to God are most strikingly displayed.

Tithing and sacrificial offering certainly were a part of worship, and the means of providing for the poor and those whose role was to maintain the acts of religious worship by which Yahweh was brought close to his people; but they were equally a recognition that all the produce of the land belonged to God, and that the firstfruits and the best of the animals supported by it were his by right. The tithe was a token that *all* belonged to God. Then the seventh day of rest was not only set aside for worship; it was a recognition that the beneficent provision of the land depended on the grace and blessing of God, and not upon the amount of work that was expended by man. Leviticus 25 and 26 encapsulate the significance of the sabbath. The seventh fallow year was to be a rest for the land and an experience of God's bountiful and gracious provision for his obedient people without their expending effort in meeting their needs. The fiftieth year was to be both a similar exercise of trust in God, with no less a glorious experience of sheer grace, and a time at which the basic resource — the land itself — was to be redistributed in accord with the original patrimony. This prevented the accumulation of the land as a resource in the hands of a few individuals. Thus God provides a way of life both for man and for nature; and so it is offered in chapter 26. Obedience brings fruitful blessing; disobedience an unchecked outworking of the consequences of the fall. For nature, however, the further judgment will produce the rest that man refused to give it, for it will "*enjoy* its sabbaths" when the disobedient nation is removed from it by the chastening hand of God (26:34-35). And, remarkably, even wild animals are to participate in the joy of the sabbath (25:7).

Thus the principal themes become intertwined and linked into an interactive development. For his chosen people God the Lord provides a land which is to yield superabundantly to meet in bountiful excess all of their needs; but that rich provision is realised only through obedience to the total requirements of the appropriate response to the redemptive acts of God in the deliverance from Egypt. Those requirements are not only religious, but also moral, embracing not only the relation of man to God, and man to man, but also man to nature. The care of God the Lord for his non-human creation in itself, independent of man, is also integral to the exquisite and intricate conflation of the major subjects of the initial exposition.

The glorious promise of benevolent and equitable material prosperity is thus offered freely out of God's grace and love for his people, but it can only be experienced and enjoyed by acting on the promise and responding to it in the way set out. On both counts the people of God fail. On reaching the border of the land they refuse to enter in the strength of Yahweh, the reality of which is the corollary of the promise (Deut.1:6-2:46). After forty years of wandering in the wilderness they enter the land but do not possess it completely, and despite their protestations of faithfulness to Yahweh, they quickly succumb to the allurements of the land (Josh.24:14-27; Jdg.2:6-15). God's redemptive acts through the judges he raises up are repeated frequently, but in every case sooner or later moral declension follows, and the fruits of the land are taken away by fresh oppressors. The repeated formulae in the book of Judges are: "The Israelites did evil in the sight of the Lord ... he gave them into the hands of their enemies ... when they cried out ... he raised up a deliverer ... the land had peace ... once again they did evil ..." (Jdg.3:7-12). The gloomy conclusion to the book is: "In those days ... everyone did as he saw fit." (21:25). The harsh minor key subject is dominant. And the land suffered as well as the people.

God then raised up a deliverer comparable to Moses in stature — Samuel, "attested as a prophet of the Lord", to whom he "revealed himself ... through his word" (1 Sam.3:20-21). He established the coherence of the nation, reformed the worship of Yahweh, instituted

110

the prophetic office which was later to be such a significant element in the life of Israel, and, like Moses, became the agent of God's revelation of his will to his people. And the land became the undisputed possession of God's people under Samuel's God-given wise authority (7:13-17). Not content with God's governance, and casting envious eyes at the peoples round about, the people of God make the sins and misdemeanours of Samuel's sons the reason for asking for a king (1 Sam.8:1-5). Their request is granted by God, but the social and agricultural consequences are clearly set out; all the compassionate provisions of Leviticus 25 are finally set aside. The rich will become richer and the poor poorer, and the resources of the land will be inequitably distributed with increasing starkness. But the reason for such developments is not only social and economic, it is the implicit rejection of Yahweh as their leader in battle and the substitution of a human leader (8:10-20). In a fallen society and a fallen nature such a change can only presage disaster, for God's land is laid open to conquest by his enemy. The second subject becomes even more dissonant and bleak in its dominance of the development, for such is the theme of much of the subsequent history recorded and commented upon in the Old Testament. Saul, initially strong and successful, sinks into madness and megalomania. David is raised up by God and under him the land of the people of God expands to its greatest extent, but even he, by adultery and murder, and weakness in his old age, makes a contribution to the decline. Absalom was the fruit of his adulterous marriage with Maacah, and exploited the weakness of David's later years. The bitter conflict concerning the succession of Solomon to the kingship was a direct consequence of David's behaviour as a typical king in that cultural milieu. Solomon taxed and oppressed the people to finance the building of the temple — and his own house and palaces. In his trade agreement with Hiram, king of Tyre, the hills of Lebanon were denuded of their magnificent cedar forests over large areas, which have never returned to their former glory. Rehoboam, an arrogant fool, brought about the division of the kingdom, and therefore of the land as well as the people. Thereafter the story in both Israel and Judah is dominated almost completely by the second subject. Only a few kings, like Hezekiah and pre-eminently Josiah, disturb the pattern of developing wickedness, oppression, and conformity to the ways of the surrounding nations and tribes. The people of God become the people of mammon, indistinguishable from those who did not know God the Lord. Judgment falls. First the northern kingdom and then the southern fall and the people are carried into captivity. And the land enjoys its sabbaths for 700 years — ten sabbaths and one full jubilee. God judges his people but has compassion on his land.

Recapitulation
Bursting into this solemn sequence of rebellion and increasing

conformity to the world at intervals, producing light and hope, are two other themes which begin to recapitulate the major themes of the exposition in Genesis 1 to 3. On the one hand there is the glorious nature poetry found in some of the Psalms (e.g. Ps.19 & Ps.104), in Job (especially chs. 38 to 41), and Isaiah, where so often in the later chapters the prophet skilfully employs vivid natural images to reinforce his message of hope (40:3-8,11-26; 41:17-20; 43:18-21; 44:24-28; 45:12-13,18-19; 55:10-13; *inter alia*). The other theme is the prophetic voice promising both judgment and forgiveness in response to repentance, in which so often the unfruitfulness of the land is linked with the gross sins of the people — spiritual and physical adultery, oppression of the weak and the poor, of the alien and the stranger, and the sensual luxury of the effete rich (Hos.2:9-15; 4:1-3,10-12; 8:7-10; 13:15; Joel 1:2-12,16-20; 2:18-27; 3:19-21; Amos 6:1-7; 9:11-15; Micah 2:8-16; 6:9-15; 7:1-6; *inter alia*). Even after the return from exile in fulfilment of God's promise the link between the fruitfulness of the land and the devotion and singlemindedness of the people of God is quite explicit (Hag.1:5-11; 2:15-19).

The former theme is a bold and transformed restatement of the first subject from the exposition. God the Lord is the creator and sustainer of all that is; it exists for his glory and pleasure; he alone knows and controls it in all its intricate, elegant and beautiful complexity, and its awesome, colossal and terrifying magnificence. More than that, nature, inarticulate, even inanimate, as it is, not only glorifies God by its very existence, but also *utters* his praise — the heavens *declare* his glory, the skies *proclaim* his work, daily they *pour forth speech* (Ps.19:1-4). Man, whom God created to be the articulate high priest of creation, as George Herbert expresses it, is deaf to their voice, blind to their proclamation, but God hears, God sees, and his heart is thrilled by the glorious harmony and counterpoint of that praise. But man needs the law of the Lord to revive his deaf, blind, dead soul, before he can truly participate in, indeed lead, that paean of praise (Ps.19:7-10). The response to that law is repentance and faith, and thus it links into the second theme, the proclamation of the prophets. In the exposition man is given the responsibility of both caring for and tilling the land; the first surely is the seed motif for his God-given role as leader of the praise and worship of nature, and the second equally surely is the motif from which the prophetic linking of the fruitfulness of the land with the obedience of the chosen people. But the pervasiveness of the second subject makes it impossible for fallen man to fulfil either without response to the law of God in repentance and faith.

The tension between the first subject and the second is still present, stark and unresolved. Repentance and faith are essentially subjective responses on the part of man to objective moral and ritual law, to an ultimately unattainable prescription of perfection, under the old dispensation of God's covenant of grace. The realisation dawns on his inspired servants that God must act objectively in order to change the whole set of disturbed relationships. Mere return from exile in humility and singleminded worship of Yahweh is not enough; it alone cannot rectify that which is wrong with man and nature. So God will create a new heart in man, write his law in their hearts, and create a new heavens and a new earth in which righteousness dwells, fully, permanently, and without any antagonistic forces (Ps.51:10; Jer.31:23-34; Isa.11:6-9; 65:17-25). Such a free, sovereign, gracious act of God relates not to man alone, but to nature in itself, and in man's use of it, and is associated with the coming of the righteous Branch springing from the root of the old Israel, the vine of God; with the coming of the Messiah, who is both Lord and King, and Suffering Servant, despised and rejected by men. During the exile and after the return the vision is amplified and embraces the creation of a new Jerusalem, and a new land with an equitable distribution of resources (Ezek. chs. 40 to 48). Thus the symphony moves towards its glorious and divinely ingenious climactic final resolution of the tension between the first subject and the second. To it everything that has gone before has been moving; from it all that follows is derived.

Climax and New Development

The divine composer's act of resolution is as simple as it is profound, as completely perfect as it is totally effective. He becomes part of his creation. God takes upon himself full humanity. By the miraculous conception in the womb of the virgin Mary, with her full consent and co-operation, the Eternal Word experiences gestation, birth, childhood, adolescence, and maturation as a man. He knows what it means to live in a fallen world, a degenerate and oppressed society, and an environment subject to futility. He reveals a deep understanding of nature both in itself and in man's use of the resources of the earth; his Father clothes the simple wild flowers so lavishly that all the expensive finery of Solomon is dowdy by comparison, and his care and concern extends even to the most insignificant and common of his creatures. He feeds the hungry who seek his word by multiplying the ordinary fruits of the earth and the waters. He stills the storm and blights the fig tree. He heals the sick and recreates the minds and bodies of the handicapped. He promises that those who seek God's kingdom and make his will the way and goal of their lives need have no anxiety about material needs, for God himself will provide all these abundantly. As he rides into Jerusalem to claim his kingdom, the very stones would burst forth in praise if children were silent. Everything he does echoes the themes of the recapitulation.

All this, however wonderful, is but a prelude to the real glory, the proper climax. The deepest, the root tension has yet to be gathered into himself and finally resolved, completely and for eternity. He moves deliberately and with complete control towards the ultimate clash with the second subject which has seemed to dominate the whole symphony for so long. At the moment he decides he subjects himself, apparently, to the final triumph of that second jarring, jagged, dissonant, gloomy theme. He gives himself up to death, the sacrament of sin. But in so doing he takes into himself all the evil and futility of nature as well as all the sin and rebellion of man, and, because that second subject has no content in itself and can exist only as the antithesis of the first, it is overcome and transformed and revealed for what it truly is, a subtle inversion of the first subject. It is none-the-less potent and powerful, real and pervasive. Its present power is residual, for the vindication of the victory is to be discerned in the resurrection, the trumpet call of the fulfilment of the promise implicit in the five-note motif contained in the first statement of the second subject: 'he will crush your head' (Gen.3:15). Since those climactic events occurred in which the people of God and the whole created universe were fully redeemed objectively and in fact by the sovereign grace of God, the ultimate consummation of the symphony is sure and certain, and the content of the triumphant coda is known, for the composer has revealed that too. While now the people of God, his Church, work, wait, and watch, in the light and power of those events through the inspiration and activity of the Holy Spirit, so the whole created order also waits and groans and travails until all the sons of God are brought to birth in Christ in this present marred and mutilated creation (Rom.8:18-25). The living presence of God, the Holy Spirit in his people and in his creation is the guarantee of the final outcome, for in Christ his people were 'chosen ... before the creation of the world; they have redemption through his blood; and they know the mystery of his will ... which he purposed in Christ ... *to bring all things in heaven and on earth together under one head*, even Christ.' (Eph.1:4-10). *All things* means precisely what it says. Nothing in all creation is excluded. The divine composer has been in control of the whole symphony from before it began — the exposition of both subjects, their development, their recapitulation, their building to an incomparable, inconceivable, incredible, even impossible climax. Not only the people of God, but the whole of the natural universe, is created and redeemed, and will be perfected, in Christ, when the times have reached their fulfilment (Eph.1:10).

Coda

The people of God today live in the development which proceeds from that climax. It is no less under the control of the composer. But it is worked out towards its certain completion in a completely new context. God, the Eternal Word, has in fact become part of his creation. By taking upon himself full human nature he also takes upon himself the burden and the promise of the natural creation, for man is part of that act and activity of God. By redeeming his people through giving himself up to death, he has also redeemed the non-human

114

creation, so that it is inevitable that through long ages since it was 'subjected to frustration ... not through its own choice but by God's will, it should not only groan in pain, but also wait in eager expectation, for its full liberation from bondage to decay into the glorious liberty of the sons of God' (Rom.8:19-21). For the redemption of the sons of God, though accomplished, is not yet fully applied, for the people of God also groan with nature as they wait eagerly for the redemption of their bodies. (Rom.8:22-23). Christ Jesus in his resurrection body is the firstfruits of that new creation, not only of the sons of God who already have the firstfruits of the Spirit, but also of the whole of nature, the total universe of the original creation (1 Cor.15:20-28, 42-49).

Thus the beloved apostle at the completion of the revelation of God in Scripture can look with absolute confidence to that new creation, to a new heavens and a new earth, just as the blessed seer had done more than eight centuries before (Rev.21:1-5; Isa.65:17-25). The blazing reality of that glorious work of God will make that reality in which God's people now live seem but a dream, ephemeral and transparent, insubstantial and insignificant. And onto that earth to people it comes the Holy City, the bride of Christ — that is the completed and perfected people of God, living in the close, unbreakable, gracious bonds of a community of divine love (Rev.21:9-14). The symphony began in a garden set apart from the old creation for the care and use of man; the symphony ends in a city in which the people of God live in perfect community centred on God and the Lamb, set in a new heavens and a new earth. The parallel between Genesis 1 and 2, and Revelation 21 and 22 can scarcely be missed. There are five elements common to both. First, the presence of minerals and precious stones, but in the apocalypse they are not simply present, but used; second, the abundance of flowing water, but in the latter picture, flowing through the centre of the city from the throne of God; third, the presence of the tree of life, but in Revelation not a single specimen, but a forest on both sides of the river; fourth, the presence of God in person, but in the city not only the centre and focus of it, but also the centre of worship, and there as the Lord God Almighty *and the Lamb*, the Eternal Word in his human form with the glory of his sacrifice indelibly imprinted upon him; and fifth, the people of God dwell in the city to serve him (Rev.21:11-21; 22:1-2; 21:22-23; 22:3). And light is unnecessary because the source of all light dwells within and his glory and that of the Lamb provides a brilliant effulgence of dazzling purity in which his servants bask. And the link to both dispensations of the covenant of grace is to be seen in the gates and the foundations of the city — the twelve tribes of the old Israel, and the twelve apostles of the new Israel (21:12-14). The coda thus encapsulates the whole symphony; the Lord of the symphony will come to complete it:

'Behold, I am coming soon! ... I, Jesus, have sent my messenger to give you all this testimony for the churches. I am the Root and the

Offspring of David, and the bright Morning Star.' (22:7,12,16). I am coming soon! — to compose and conduct a new, unimaginably glorious symphony of creation, redemption and glory?

Amen. Come, Lord Jesus.

THE CHILDREN FOR CHRIST

His Covenant Seed and their Covenant Sign

J. DOUGLAS MACMILLAN

A powerful and attractive aspect of the ministry which this book celebrates has been its focus on the welfare and status of the church's children. It has been bold enough, and Biblical enough, to see them not merely as the church of tomorrow but as the church of today.

As the years went by it seemed to many of Mr Still's friends that his appreciation of federal or covenantal theology enlarged itself and that it was his grasp of the place of children within that theology, and the practical questions which flow from it, that imparted a vital dimension to his ministry and the congregational life which it produced. Children were restored to the place which they had once held in Scottish churches; federal theology was not only believed, it was practised.

The healthy emphasis on 'family' religion which has characterised Gilcomston, generations of the congregation's children retained in the Christian faith, and published work on infant baptism are indicators of the prominence given in his ministry by Mr Still to the Biblical teaching on how the church should care for the children born within her fold. As one who shares his convictions and admires his action in this area, I would like to explore, by way of tribute, some aspects of the Bible's teaching on the children of believers, as covenant theology interprets these, and in particular, their covenantal right to the sacrament of baptism.

Getting the Question in Focus

It is a fact that no single passage or text in the New Testament can be pointed to as affording undisputed evidence that the New Testament practice was the baptism of children.

The fact that we are without express command to baptise children and that we are unable to cite any explicit case of infant baptism from the New Testament does not, however, mean that we must immediately abandon it. That would be no answer to the problem at all. It would merely be a simplistic solution to a difficulty which, viewed from a wider perspective, proves to be more apparent than real.

The first step in assessing the reality of the difficulty is to set it in context. Is it in fact the case that whenever there is no express or explicit injunction requiring a duty to be performed then that duty is either unlawful or may safely be neglected?

That question brings us face to face with two principles that must govern and regulate our approach to the Biblical teaching on any

117

specific question of Christian doctrine or Christian duty. These principles are given clear and cogent expression in the Westminster Confession of Faith where it is declared that, 'The whole counsel of God, concerning all things necessary for his own glory, man's salvation, faith and life, is either expressly set down in Scripture, or *by good and necessary consequence may be deduced from scripture*' (Westminster Confession of Faith, 1:6 italics ours). In his comment on this article of the Confession, Robert Shaw sets out its implications in a way that really dissolves the difficulty we have posited. He says, 'We do not insist that every article of religion is contained in Scripture in so many words; but we hold that conclusions fairly deduced from the declarations of the Word of God are as truly parts of divine revelation as if they were expressly taught in the Sacred Volume'.[1] Two principles, then, one of 'Express command', the other of 'Necessary inference', are to be applied in establishing the Biblical basis of any Christian doctrine or duty. And where one fails in any specific instance, as the first one does in the case of infant baptism, then the second one must become the determinative factor in deciding the issues at stake in that particular instance. Into this category, then, of 'good and necessary consequence', the New Testament itself forces us to go with our study of the Biblical basis of infant baptism. This fact must also be accounted for, and our evaluation of what is called the 'New Testament silence' on the issue, must take account of its historical and theological context. The sacraments were not instituted in a vacuum but against the background provided by Old Testament teaching and practice. Further, the Bible itself makes it clear that the sacraments are to be understood within a covenantal framework.

Having clarified the principles that must guide our approach to the Biblical teaching on our topic and having identified the context from within which that teaching may be traced we can proceed to set out the data which provide the Biblical mandate for child-baptism.

Preliminary Considerations

Before we do this, however, I wish to pave the way into that study by stating some considerations that bear upon an evaluation of these data and the conclusions to which they point. These are merely the brief statement of certain concepts of covenantal theology which can be established on Scriptural teaching but which, here, in the interests of brevity, are elucidated only in their immediate bearing upon our theme:

(i) *The Unity of the Old and New Testament Scriptures*

Each of these sheds light upon the teaching of the other and both are so linked, as to make one, indivisible, rule of faith and life for the Christian church.

---

1. Robert Shaw, *The Reformed Faith. An Exposition of the Westminster Confession of Faith,* repr. Edinburgh, 1974, p. 16.

(ii)   *The Essential Unity of the Covenant of Grace*

The covenant administered under the Gospel is the same covenant in its essential terms as that revealed in various outward forms to the church of God under the Old Testament dispensation. It is the final unfolding of what was embraced in the first promise to post-fall Adam, and, its progressive revelation under various forms to Noah, Abraham, Moses and the prophets, can be regarded as the republication and the amplification of God's initial free promise of grace through the one covenant Mediator, the Lord Jesus Christ. This unity is given express statement by Paul when he says that, 'The Gospel was preached before unto Abraham' (Galatians 3:8), and when he elaborates that by going on to say, 'The covenant confirmed of God in Christ was given to Abraham four hundred and thirty years before the giving of the Law' (Galatians 3:17). 'Language', as Bannerman remarks, 'fitted to mark both the identity of the covenant of Abraham with the Gospel covenant, and its independence of the Mosaic ceremonial institutions'.[2]

(iii)   *The Unity of the Church of God in Old and New Testament Times*

God has had a people on earth since the Fall. These people were graciously dealt with by God on the basis of the covenant which can be regarded as the charter of the church in every age. Those who have made up the church in every age have, by the same God, been called from the same lost state to the same Saviour and Mediator, Jesus Christ. Since the beginning he has been the Prophet, Priest and King of the church. The church in the days of Noah — in the days of Abraham — the church in the days of Moses — and the church under the Gospel — while it was formed in various outward patterns according to the particular dictates of the developing covenant revelation was, in all its essential elements, one and the same Church. Galatians 3:7 reads, 'Understand, then, that those who believe are children of Abraham'. This establishes the essential spritual relationship which exists between New Testament believers and Abraham. Verse 9 goes on to say, 'So those who have faith are blessed along with Abraham, the man of faith,' and this establishes that the New Testament church inherits and enjoys the very same blessings that were Abraham's in the covenant. And the essential unity between the two is brought to the fore yet again when Paul states, 'If you belong to Christ, then you are Abraham's seed, and heirs according to the promise' (Galatians 3:29). That it was essentially the same Church even under the period of the Mosaic ceremonial is evident from the speech of Stephen in Acts 7:38 where, having quoted the prophecy of Moses concerning the coming prophet, he says, 'This is he, that was in the church in the wilderness' (A.V).

(iv)   *The Importance of the Family Unit in God's Dealings with Men*

Man was created in the 'Image and Likeness of God'. That involved

---

2. James Bannerman, *The Church of Christ,* repr. Edinburgh, 1974, ii, p. 70.

not merely man's individual personality but his circle of relationship with his kin. God himself ever exists in the fellowship of trinity and he it was who 'set the solitary in families' (Psalm 68:6). The trinity is the prototype of the family and, in this sense, the fact that the family fellowship was the sphere in which man was to bring forth children in his own likeness, thus imaging forth the creative power of God, makes it eminently fitting that the family should be the basic unit in God's covenant purposes for man; a unit of which the father is the representative and head.

(v)   *The Covenant of Grace under the Old Testament made Provision for the Children of Believing Parents*

From its first free promise of grace to Adam, every fresh revelation of the covenant has highlighted this fact. An early instance in Scripture of the child's covenant status being in direct relation to its parent's faith, is that of Noah. His salvation was one of the first great illustrations of God's redemptive grace at work in a sinful world. In that act he demonstrated what was to be one of the great principles of his covenant activities towards man. The Genesis record makes clear the principle upon which God acted in saving, not only Noah, but his family from destruction. 'The Lord then said to Noah, "Go into the ark, you and your whole family, because I have found you righteous in this generation"' (Genesis 7:1). The New Testament commentary on that act of God's grace confirms the principle of operation very simply but altogether sufficiently, 'By faith Noah prepared an ark, to the saving of his house' (Hebrews 11:7 A.V. Note also 1 Peter 3:20-21). It is beyond question that it was upon the basis of the father's faith that this whole family was saved. Noah is thus made a witness to future ages that the faith of a believing parent secures a blessing, not for himself alone, but for the children as well. It is no surprise to us then, that, when the covenant was established, in more fully elaborated terms, with Abraham, its provisions include not merely Abraham, but his children as well. 'I will establish my covenant as an everlasting covenant between me and you and your descendants after you for the generations to come, to be your God and the God of your descendants after you' (Genesis 17:7).

Some Necessary Consequences

Now, the positions which we have set out thus far, along with the bare indications of the line that the establishment of their full Scriptural validity would follow, dictate to us, certain 'good and necessary consequences' which can now be asserted and supported by various strands of Biblical teaching.

(i)   *The first Assertion which we make is, that the Old Testament must be brought to bear upon the Issue of Infant Baptism*

It is rich in its teaching of the place and privilege of believer's children in the church of God during that dispensation. It was over against that teaching and under its guiding influence that the New Testament church was established. The Old Testament provided the norms by which the New Testament church organised its life and expressed its faith. To confine the study of infant baptism to the New Testament Scriptures — as is so often urged upon us — merely because baptism is a New Testament ordinance is to beg a high and vital part of the question. It is to leave out of consideration a fund of evidence which is absolutely germane to the Biblical basis of baptism, and more particularly so when the baptism in question is that of the children of believers. Here we must insist, and insist in the strongest possible way, that, 'All Scripture is God-breathed and is useful for teaching... for correcting and training in righteousness' (2 Timothy 3:16). The unity of the covenant and the unity of the church of God established through the covenant, demands that the place of children in the Old Testament church regulate our whole approach to, and understanding of, the place of children in the New Testament church.

(ii) *The second Assertion we make is, that the Covenant of Grace has always included Infants in its Provisions, and still does under the Gospel*

Each time the covenant was revealed to man it included the child with the parent. This was the case, as we have seen, with Adam, Noah and Abraham. It was also the case with Israel through Moses. 'All of you are standing today in the presence of the Lord your God- ...together with your children...in order to enter into a covenant with the Lord your God...to confirm you this day as his people, that he may be your God as he promised you and as he swore to your fathers, Abraham, Isaac and Jacob' (Deuteronomy 29:10-13). The very same keynote was struck in the opening sermon of the Gospel era. Men were exhorted to believe for the specific reason that, 'the promise is for you and your children' (Acts 2:39). At the beginning of the New Testament church we find that the title-deeds of its covenant life ensure, still, a covenant status for children of those who believe.

The nature and character of that status is confirmed for us in an interesting answer which Paul gives to a question which was posed to him by the church at Corinth. His reply to the problem given him is to be found in 1 Corinthians 7:14, where we read, 'For the unbelieving husband has been sanctified through his wife, and the unbelieving wife has been sanctified through her believing husband. Otherwise your children would be unclean, but as it is they are holy.' The word *holy* is the very same word that he uses earlier for Church *members* and which we translate, *'saints'*. The primary meaning of the word is 'to be set apart', and it is invariably used in Scripture of something set apart to God. It was used, for example, of Israel in the sense of their being a people set apart to God. They were a *holy* people, not because every individual amongst them was regenerate in heart, but simply because they were set apart by the covenant of grace to a holy purpose among the nations of the earth. This meant that they had special privileges through the covenant, one of which was, for instance, that 'they have been entrusted with the very words of God' (Romans 3:2).

Now the context of 1 Corinthians 7:14 makes it clear that Paul was dealing with the specific problems of Christian converts married to unbelievers and the status that children of such a marriage should have in the church. Were they to be accepted with the believing parent or were they cast off with the unbelieving parent? Paul declares that the unbelieving partner and the children were 'set apart' to God in virtue of the faith of the believing partner and parent. He is not, of course, teaching that the children of such a marriage are 'saved'; but he does say that the faith and church membership of one parent sets them apart, and the term he uses implies some spiritual privilege. In this lies the whole force of his statement. For a people familiar with the covenantal teaching of the Old Testament this, of course, made perfect sense and Paul takes this familiarity for granted. His statement answered what was to them a very real problem. But outwith the framework of covenant principles it is difficult, not only to make complete sense of Paul's answer, but even to appreciate the problem to which his answer was the reassuring solution. Within that framework, this Scripture simply reaffirms the spiritual privileges of children who have even one believing parent. It demonstrates also that the children of believers are in a different category, respecting their relationship to God, than are children who have no Christian parentage. 'There is,' says John Murray in a comment on this passage, 'a status or condition which can be characterised as "holiness", which belongs to children in virtue of a parental relationship.' And, he goes on to say, 'It is a "holiness" that evinces the operation of the covenant and representative principle'.[3]

(iii) *The third Assertion is that: the Church of God, which is the same under both Dispensations, has always included Infants among its Members, and still does*

There is no doubt that the church in the Old Testament was the church of Christ just as really as the church of the New Testament is. In prophecy, type, symbol and promise, faith laid hold of Christ and the benefits which, in the fullness of time, would be actualised by his atoning sacrifice. The spiritual realities enjoyed were, in essence, those which the believer under the Gospel enjoys. It is equally sure that into the Abrahamic church infants, as well as their parents, were admitted as members. Circumcision was given as the seal of the covenant and as the badge of membership in the Church which began to take a formal, outward structure from the Abrahamic covenant. This import of circumcision is not to be traced to the Mosaic administration of the covenant, but to the Abrahamic. Jesus said to the Jews that this ordinance 'did not come from Moses, but from the patriarchs' (John 7:22).

In the New Testament there is not the slightest indication of such a

3. John Murray, *Christian Baptism*, Philadelphia, 1962, p. 68.

change with regard to the place of children in the church — but rather the opposite. Let us glance at some of the evidence that supports that claim, noting two things in particular.

First, Jesus and the little ones. It is reported in all three of the synoptic Gospels that Jesus rebuked his disciples because they hindered little ones from coming to him. Luke makes it clear that 'People were bringing babies to Jesus' (Luke 18:15), and the word he uses to describe those so brought is *brephe-brephos* which does, indeed, mean infants or babies. Note that all three Gospels mention that Jesus 'laid hands upon them' or 'touched them' (Matthew 19:15; Mark 10:16; Luke 18:15); that Mark says, 'he took the children in his arms, put his hands on them and blessed them' (Mark 10:16). And Matthew makes it clear that there was a very specific purpose in the minds of the parents who brought these infants to Jesus, when he gives the reason, thus, 'For him to place his hands on them and pray for them' (Matthew 19:13). This is all too often understood as a kindly sentimental 'recognition' of children by the Lord. It was far more than that. Laying on of his hands — prayer — taking up in his arms — blessing — these are the terms used, and they are each significant. The words, 'Do not hinder them, for the kingdom of God belongs to such as these' (Matthew 19:14) seal the solemn nature of what Jesus did. While we do not rest infant baptism upon these passages we do claim that, at the very least, they are strongly indicative of continuing covenant favour for little ones, and mark their standing in the new administration of the covenant as no different from what it had been in the old. They make clear also, as G. W. Bromiley puts it, that Jesus 'does not seem to share the rationalistic view that the Holy Spirit cannot do his work of illumination and regeneration except in those who have at least the beginnings of an adult understanding. He does not endorse the idea that small children are not the proper subjects of his kingdom and therefore of the sacraments or signs of the kingdom'.[4]

Secondly, the place that Paul gives to children in his letters (e.g. Ephesians 6:1-4; Colossians 3:20). Paul addresses children as though they not only have a place in the church but in the discipline and privileges which are exercised in and by the church. In Colossians, where he is exhorting certain types of behaviour upon church members and where the members are classified — wives — husbands — masters — servants, one group is, 'children' and they, like the others, are exhorted to do all, 'In the name of the Lord Jesus, giving thanks to God the Father through him' (Colossians 3:17).

These citations are perfectly natural and easy to understand given the continuity of the New Testament church with the Old, and the inclusion of children of the believers amongst its membership. The children of Christian parents, in virtue of belonging to the believing community and sealed with the sign of the covenant, are to be taught

4. G. W. Bromiley, *Children of Promise*, Edinburgh, 1979, p. 5.

the covenant obligation and privilege of obedience to parents in the Lord.

(iv) *The fourth Assertion is that: the Ordinance of Outward Admission to the Church has not changed, in its Inward Character and Meaning, under the Gospel.* Here we identify as essentially one and the same in their use, meaning and character, the Old Testament rite of circumcision and the New Testament rite of baptism. This lies close to the crux of our entire discussion and if it can be shown that the two ordinances held the same place, meant the same thing, and performed the same function, in the one church of God, under both dispensations of the covenant of grace, then it is difficult to evade the conclusion that the one ought to be administered to the infant members of the one church under the last dispensation, as the other was under the previous one. Three points can be made.

First, both ordinances signal membership of the one church. That circumcision was the ordinance admitting to outward membership of the Old Testament church will not be questioned. There was no access to the privileges of that church except through the door of circumcision. By express command all infants born into the fellowship of that church must be circumcised. In virtue of its birth and the privileges that carried, the infant was sealed in circumcision as a member of the visible church. And it was as a member of the church that it was ceremonially, and spiritually, qualified to receive the outward privileges, and the inward blessings that were held out, or conveyed, through that church as a means of grace. There was no further qualifying ceremony of admission. This is indicative of the fact that, while circumcision was the outward badge of the visible church, it was also what it had been to Abraham himself in its first administration, the seal of admission to the true Gospel church.

Baptism as the seal of membership in the New Testament church requires no elaborate proof. The great commission along with the apostolic practice with converts to the faith amply demonstrates it to be so. As seals of membership in the church of God, circumcision and baptism perform the same function and mean the same thing. They hold in this respect one and the same place, at different periods in time, in one and the same church. The Biblical affinity between the two goes even further, though, as our second point shows.

Secondly, circumcision and baptism are signs and seals of the same covenant blessings. The great blessings held out in the covenant of grace are justification from the guilt of sin and renewal by the Holy Spirit. That circumcision was expressive of justification by faith and sealed it to the true believer is stated by Paul: 'And he (i.e. Abraham) received the sign of circumcision, a seal of the righteousness that he had by faith while he was still uncircumcised' (Romans 4:11). That circumcision was expressive of heart renewal and heart-cleansing is also clear: 'The Lord your God will circumcise your hearts and the hearts of your descendants, so that you may love him with all your heart and with all your soul and live' (Deuteronomy 30:6). The inward reality symbolised by circumcision was a work of saving grace in the heart. New Testament usage confirms this. 'A man,' says Paul, 'is a Jew if he is one inwardly; and circumcision is circumcision of the heart, by the Spirit, not by the written code' (Romans 2:29). It is hardly necessary to elaborate the fact that these same, inward, spiritual blessings are deeply embedded in the meaning of New Testament baptism.

Thirdly, baptism replaces circumcision as the covenant sign of inward renewal, in the New Testament era. Read against its Old Testament background the New Testament makes it clear that sacraments which Christ instituted, baptism and the Lord's supper, correspond to the two covenantal signs of the Old Testament; the Lord's supper to the passover, baptism to circumcision. The point of discontinuity between the old signs and the new is self-evident and interprets the replacement for us. The old signs both involved blood-shedding, a feature which pointed forward, in type and promise, to the atoning work of Christ. By way of contrast, the new signs look backward to the 'one sacrifice for sin' (Hebrews 10:12) which has taken place and the fulfilment of which is emphasised by the bloodless nature of the signs. This outward discontinuity emphasises, not the disjunction between the facts symbolised but, in a very positive way, their spiritual continuity.

The continuity, in both cases, is spelled out in the New Testament in a clear way. The institution of the Lord's supper marks it quite strongly but, Paul actually spells it out for us, 'Christ our passover lamb has been sacrificed for us' (1 Corinthians 5:7). In the case of the other signs, which are our particular interest here, the link is established by Paul in Colossians 2:11-12. Expositors differ in their detailed interpretations of this passage but the focal fact it proclaims is quite clear. Over against those wishing believers to have the Old Testament sign of the covenant, circumcision, Paul urges, very cogently, that they have already been circumcised: 'In him you were also circumcised, in the putting off of the sinful nature, not with a circumcision done by the hands of men but with the circumcision done by Christ' (Colossians 2:11). If we ask, when was that inward work sealed to these believers the answer is emphatic — 'having been buried with him in baptism and raised with him through your faith' (Colossians 2:12). In terms of the Old Testament teaching it would hardly be possible to find a more positive rebuttal of the need for circumcision or to find a more accurate and fitting description of what had happened to those people than is couched in the phrase 'the circumcision of Christ'.

(v) *The fifth Assertion is that: the Principle of the Admission of Children as Church Members was, and still is, the Covenant Status of their Parents*

It was to the faith of the parent that the promise was made, and the sign given in the cases of Noah and Abraham. Right through the history of the Old Testament church the family unit was the pivot around which God's dealings in covenant grace turned. The promise was unvaried in its terms — 'you and your seed'. The faith of the parent conditioned the Godward standing of the child. In the light of that fact it is instructive to note the precise vocabulary used by Peter when the covenant terms are republished to the New Testament church. The vocabulary of Acts 2:38-39 is that which any man would use in summarising the covenant terms proclaimed to Abraham in Genesis 17. There, the covenant promise of God embraced three things. Blessing to himself; blessing to his seed; blessing to many nations. How succinctly and cogently Peter puts these three elements forward, then, as he unfolds the covenant promise and holds out to his hearers the blessing which it assures to repentance and faith. 'The promise,' he says, 'is to you, and to your children, and to all that are afar off.' In Acts 2:39, then, it is clear that infants are not only placed in the same relation to their parent's faith as they are in Genesis 17, but that they are placed in precisely the same relation to baptism as they were to circumcision; and they are placed there by the identical terms of an identical covenant promise.

Concerns in New Testament Practice

Having looked at some of the basic factors which have to come into our consideration of child baptism and at the way in which these establish the correlation between the Old Testament covenant sign and that of the New Testament, it remains now to look a little more closely at what did take place in the New Testament church. Do the baptisms spoken of there strengthen or weaken the link we have been following? Do the New Testament facts encourage us to see baptism as a suitable replacement for and fulfilment of the sign of circumcision? Of twelve cases of baptism cited in the New Testament — and only twelve are mentioned out of the thousands that must have taken place — no less than four — perhaps five — are cases of what we generally refer to as 'house-hold baptism' but which, for reasons that will follow, I prefer to call *'family* baptisms'.

The fact that at least four out of twelve baptisms are recorded as taking place within a family situation is interesting on statistical grounds alone. But it is even more so on linguistic grounds.

The New Testament uses two Greek words for house and household — *oikos, oikia*. In every instance in the New Testament it is said that the *oikos* was baptised, never the *oikia*. This is significant because of the different connotation of the two words. The literal meaning of *oikos* is the inside of the house, or the rooms in it which are used by the family which lives there. The literal meaning of *oikia* is the ground around the house — or the immediate setting of the house. Both words, however, seem to have a similarly differentiated figurative meaning. Figuratively, *oikos* is used of the immediate family, *oikia* of other persons who go to make up the wider household, or of people who are assembled there in a meeting. A house, in this sense of *oikos*, implies family lineage, but the figurative distinction between 'house' and 'household' is not so clear to us in English — if, indeed, it is there at all — and so the distinction tends to be obscured in our English translations. The Greek text of Acts 16:31-33 illustrates the distinction quite clearly. 'And they said, Believe on the Lord Jesus Christ, and thou shalt be saved, and thy house' — and there 'house' is *oikos*; then, in verse 32 we read, 'And they spake unto him the word of the Lord, and to those that were in his house' — *en tae oikia*. And then when it comes to the actual baptism, and to those who were baptised, they are denominated, *autos kai hoi autou pantes* — 'he and all his'. Now, had the English translation taken note of this distinction and translated *oikos* as 'family' it would have followed the sense of the Greek text more closely and avoided the confusion that tends to arise in the mind of the reader about the precise connotation of 'house' and 'household'.

Noting these distinctions Dr Alan Harman goes on to say, 'It is interesting that in the two references to the family of Stephanus, in the first in 1 Corinthians 1:16 *oikos* is used, but in 1 Corinthians 16:15 ("You know the household of Stephanus, that they were the first fruits of Achaia, and that they have devoted themselves for the ministry of the saints") the wider word *oikia* appears'.[5]

Irrespective of the linguistic argument, however, the baptism of families or households provides evidence that the 'representative' or 'family' principle, so deeply embedded in Jewish practice, was in operation in the New Testament church just as it had been in the Old. That fact lends its support to our entire thesis.

Enough has probably been said to demonstrate that, 'by good and necessary consequence', a broad spectrum of Scripture teaches that infants of believers are to be admitted as members of the visible Gospel church and that the seal of their membership in that church is baptism. Let us summarise the situation, however, with a closer look at the actual instances of baptism in the New Testament and by examining the data they give us against the background of all that has been said already.

As we have seen, the New Testament gives us only twelve instances of actual baptism. Of these twelve, four are clear instances of household baptism — and, if the household of Crispus be included on the grounds of 1 Corinthians 1:14, allied with Acts 18:8, the number is five. Here the number of family baptisms is high enough to indicate such baptism as a frequent occurence in the apostolic practice and one can only agree with John Murray when he says, 'It would be practically impossible to believe that in none of these households were there any

5. Alan Harman in *Hold Fast your Confession*, ed Donald Macleod, Edinburgh, 1978, p. 209.

infants'.[6] But further, of the remaining seven cases cited, four were of 'group' or 'crowd' baptisms and the presumptive case for children being a part of any, or of all of them, is of the strongest kind. That leaves only three stated cases where we can be absolutely clear that no child was involved and where we have the baptism of individuals being baptised upon the profession of their own faith. These are, Simon of Samaria, the Ethiopian eunuch, and Saul of Tarsus. Let us note too that these were baptised within the context of a missionary situation. In a similar situation today, any paedobaptist minister or missionary would require the same profession before baptising any similar adult convert and, in such a situation, he would expect a good number of such baptisms. But, once the missionary situation was no longer the predominant one, such cases of baptism would not, in a paedobaptist church, be so frequent. And, although the New Testament writings extend for a period of more than thirty years from the inception of the Christian church, it is surely a very significant fact that not one single case of the baptisms instanced in the New Testament was that of an adult who had grown to the age of maturity within the Gospel church.

On the inference that children were baptised along with their parents the absence of 'second generation' baptism is not surprising; but apart from that thesis it is inexplicable in a record that covers the first thirty/sixty years of New Testament church-life so extensively. On the other hand, the existence of even one such instance would be a stronger counterpoint to the continuity of the covenant principle in the New Testament church than any other factor which can be brought against it. But the fact of the matter is that the baptism of people who have grown up within the church is a practice which cannot be demonstrated from the New Testament.

Finally, we must remind ourselves of the background against which the New Testament writings are to be set. They are to be set in the perspective of the total teaching of the Old Testament on the place of the child within the covenant, and within the church which the covenant terms established. Hence, it need not surprise us that none of these writings should carry an express command, or contain an explicit example, about administering the sign and seal of the covenant to the child. The Old Testament teaching was so clear, the warrant so deeply embedded in its warp and woof, that no new command was necessary. The New Testament silence at this point, far from being a weakness in the whole case, is one of its best pillars of support. The practice was perfectly clear and it was to remain what it had ever been in the covenant dealings of a gracious God with his people. The federal theology which we have inherited in Scotland provides a cogent framework within which to demonstrate that the practice of baptising the children of all Christian believers is firmly rooted in the teaching of Scripture, and that the duty of every Christian church and the privilege

6. John Murray, *op. cit.*, p. 69.

of every Christian parent as to the baptism of their children is made very clear by 'good and necessary consequence' from principles which lie richly widespread through the Old and New Testaments.

It is the unity of the covenant, taken along with the covenantal solidarity of the parent/child relationship, which establishes, we believe, the right of the believer's child to the sign and seal of the covenant just as surely in New as in Old Testament times.

The baptism of our children is a perpetual seal to us that God is not only a God to his people but also to their seed after them. When this is understood, who is the Christian parent or the Christian minister but will say, 'Can any man forbid water that these should not be baptised?' (Acts 10:47).

THE PROBLEM OF APOSTASY IN HEBREWS

HENRY A. G. TAIT

It was in Gilcomston thirty five years ago that I came to know the Lord. Among my recollections of that time are the summer evenings of 1951, the sunlight streaming through the tall west gallery windows to fall on the figure in the pulpit, as, with all his heart and soul and body, he preached through the pages of Hebrews, for — and here is a word to all preachers and a particular word of comfort to those of us who are charged from time to time with being too demonstrative — it is what I *saw* that I remember now: the grim gesture described in the air of a nail being hammered into wood that made vivid and appalling the words of the writer, 'seeing they crucify to themselves the Son of God afresh and put him to an open shame'. It was unforgettable. And now I count it a privilege far beyond my capacities to have been invited to contribute something to this book of essays being presented to William Still. What you are about to read — if you read it — ill reflects the immense honour in which I hold the man to whom I owe in my own soul and life and ministry a debt incalculable.

But to my task. Consider the case of a man we shall call John Smith. He was converted as a young man. Perhaps, in order not to prejudice matters, we ought to say that he *professed* conversion as a young man. But no one doubted at the time that it was true. The evidence was there in his changed life. The Christ-light shone in his face. He loved God's word. He loved the fellowship of the Lord's people. He had zeal and joy. He showed gifts for prayer and ministry. In course of time he was persuaded that God was calling him to fuller service. To obey was going to be costly and difficult. But the cost was embraced, and one by one the difficulties were overcome, God apparently (one might say, surely) confirming the call with his enablings and provision. The church was encouraged and rejoiced. Then came temptation, singular in its severity. John fell. In a matter of a very short time, all had been abandoned, calling, faith, profession, fellowship, all, and in their stead came an open and blatant disavowal of Christ and God, a total desertion of the church, and a full-blooded return to the ways of the world, as if the spiritual experience had never been. John was an apostate. What is to become of such in this world and the next? That is the intense problem that lies behind this study of a well known crux in the New Testament.

Most evangelicals believe that, once a man has received Christ as his Saviour, he cannot lose him. If he has chosen Christ, it is because God has first chosen him, and drawn him (John 6:44). Those whom God foreknew, he also predestined to be conformed to the image of his Son

131

. . . and those whom he predestined, he also called, and those whom he called, he also justified; and those whom he justified, he also glorified (Romans 8:29f). That is the chain of our salvation. Every link in it is wrought by God. It cannot break. Our assurance on the point is further confirmed by what Paul wrote to the Philippians, 'He who began a good work in you will bring it to completion at the day of Jesus Christ' (Philippians 1:6). Jesus said of his sheep, 'No one shall snatch them out of my hand. My Father, who has given them to me, is greater than all, and no one is able to snatch them out of my Father's hand'. (John 10:28f). We sometimes say, particularly with regard to the aged or sick of mind, 'Our hold on him may weaken and grow slack. His hold on us will be firm to the end'. Jesus said, 'Truly, truly, I say to you, he who hears my word and believes him who sent me, has eternal life; he does not come into judgment but has passed from death to life' (John 5:24). That sounds pretty conclusive. If eternal life is life without end, can it be received and then lost? Hardly: we have it forever. 'There is therefore now no condemnation to them that are in Christ Jesus' (Romans 8:1).

So the Westminster Confession of Faith can say, 'They whom God hath accepted in his Beloved, effectually called and sanctified by his Spirit, can neither totally nor finally fall away from the state of grace; but shall certainly persevere therein to the end, and be eternally saved' (Confession 17:1).

This doctrine, however, appears to sit uncomfortably alongside certain passages in the Epistle to the Hebrews. It is a discomfort that was felt very early in church history. Following Tertullian, the Novatians and the Montanists used Hebrews as warrant for the perpetual exclusion from fellowship of those deemed to have apostatised by 'sinning wilfully' after conversion even though they sought to return. And in the heat of the consequent debate those who opposed and countered that position found themselves voicing doubts as to whether Hebrews should ever have been included in the canon of the Bible at all. Down to the present time Hebrews is the book to which principal appeal is made by those in the church who teach that a real Christian can fall away and lose his salvation. There seems to be a discrepancy on this point between the teaching of Hebrews and what we understand the rest of the New Testament to be saying. To some folk in the church of course this presents no problem. The writer to the Hebrews, they would argue, was a man of clay as were the other writers of the books of the Bible. They had their own opinions and we are free to choose which opinions we will receive and which set aside.

Evangelicals do not have nor desire this dubious liberty. We are persuaded that all Scripture is inspired by God, Old Testament and New, and each Testament in all its parts. Coming, then, from God's holy mind the scriptures cannot contradict one another. They harmonise, though we may not always, in the state of our knowledge at any one time, perceive precisely how they do so.

132

We reject the 'Clay Man' as a solution to the difficulty. But three other men offer themselves; the Straw Man, the Hollow Man, and the Man of Tarnished Metal.

There are five passages in Hebrews which together present the most serious warnings in the New Testament: Hebrews 2:1-3; 3:7-4, 13; 6:4-12; 10:19-39 and 12:1-17. Of these the third and the fourth are the ones which present the major difficulty. Here is the core of them:

> It is impossible to restore again to repentance those who have once been enlightened, who have tasted the heavenly gift, and become partakers of the Holy Spirit, and have tasted the goodness of the word of God and the powers of the age to come, if they then commit apostasy, since they crucify the Son of God on their own account, and hold him up to contempt. For the land which has drunk the rain which often falls upon it, and brings forth vegetation useful to those for whose sake it is cultivated, receives a blessing from God. But if it bears thorns and thistles, it is worthless and near to being cursed: its end is to be burned. (Hebrews 6:4-8).
>
> For if we sin deliberately, after receiving the knowledge of the truth, there no longer remains a sacrifice for sins, but a fearful prospect of judgment, and a fury of fire which will consume the adversaries. A man who has violated the law of Moses dies without mercy at the testimony of two or three witnesses. How much worse punishment do you think will be deserved by the man who has spurned the Son of God, and profaned the blood of the covenant by which he was sanctified, and outraged the Spirit of grace? For we know him who said, 'Vengeance is mine, I will repay'. And again, 'The Lord will judge his people'. It is a fearful thing to fall into the hands of the living God. (Hebrews 10:29-31).

The Straw Man interpretation is that the author is speaking only hypothetically. In other words the Writer is not talking about a situation that existed or indeed could exist. He is saying, 'If it were possible for the believer to fall away, these are the fearful things which would surely befall him. So since these things would be so if you were to give up the faith, see that you stand fast!' This is the approach commended by Hewitt in the Tyndale commentary (pp 110f). 'The theory', he says, 'has much in its favour and little against it. It in no way contradicts other passages of Scripture, neither is it in conflict with the doctrine of the perseverance of the saints.'

These are virtues indeed, if of a rather negative sort, and as a way out of the difficulty this solution may commend itself to many readers, particularly if they find the alternative solutions even less acceptable.

The Hollow Man may be described in terms of the figure who appears in our Lord's interpretation of the Parable of the Sower. He is the man who, on hearing the word, immediately received it with joy but having no root within himself — or not having, as we would say, 'the root of the matter in him' — when tribulation and persecution came on account of the word, immediately fell away. Is this the man the author of Hebrews is speaking of?

In Hebrews 6:4, the man described has 'been enlightened'. That could mean 'instructed or well informed in or about the faith'. He has 'tasted the heavenly gift'. It is possible that the reference is to the

Lord's Table, or it may refer to a more general experience of or acquaintance with the gospel. John Owen points out (in his massive *Commentary on Hebrews*) that you can taste a thing but fail to go on to swallow and digest it. You can reject something of which you have made even long trial.

Hebrews 6 adds that he has 'become a partaker of the Holy Ghost'. The reference could be to his baptism, or to the laying on of hands at admission to the fellowship, or it might be to various experiences he may have had of the operations of the Holy Spirit whether of a common or a miraculous sort (and not just as an observer). He might have been an active participant. After all did not our Lord say that some would come to him at the last and say, presumably truthfully, 'Lord, Lord, did we not prophesy in your name, and cast out demons in your name, and do many mighty works in your name?' but that his response would be, 'I never knew you; depart from me you evildoers' (Matthew 7:22f). The unregenerate, it seems, could be 'partakers of the Holy Ghost'.

Further, the person in view in Hebrews 6 has 'tasted the goodness of the word of God and the powers of the age to come'. This may mean that he has heard and appreciated many sermons. He is not just a detached sermon taster, a connoisseur of the preacher's art; he has received impacts on his soul as he has listened to the truth about the Kingdom of God. He may know indeed that God himself has spoken to him personally. For all that, he may have declined to yield him his heart. Thus, inwardly and secretly, he remains unregenerate. Outwardly to the public eye, he is a Christian, for has professed Christ, associated with his people, adopted their ways, and lent his strength to the church. Consequently such a man has much to fall away from. When he defects, he brings Christ into public scorn. He has despised and rejected him, and crucified him afresh. Like that second field in the author's illustration, he took in much, of truth and good, but the fruit of faith has never really grown in his life at all. He *professed* Christ, but did not *possess* him. So not having the gift of eternal life he can fall away and die in his sins.

How does this 'Hollow Man' interpretation square with the man described in Hebrews 10? He 'received the knowledge of truth'; so surely did our man. He 'spurned the Son of God'. So did our man, for he made trial of Christ and then rejected him, tasted him and spat him out. He 'profaned the blood of the covenant by which he was sanctified'. Did our man do that? Was our man sanctified by the blood of the covenant? Can it be said that someone who professes Christ but does not possess him is sanctified by the blood? One might think not. On the other hand one might think that in that he was baptised in water outwardly and formally he was sanctified by the blood of the covenant. He was certainly seen to be so by man. He himself might even have thought he was at the time. John Brown in his *Commentary on Hebrews* appreciates this difficulty and suggests that what the words mean is, he 'profaned the blood of the covenant by which *Christ* was sanctified', that is, to his High Priestly office, or, he suggests that we depersonalise the reference and take it simply to mean 'sanctifying blood' (pp 473f).

The man described in Chapter 10 is further said to have 'outraged the Spirit of grace'. Did our man do so? Certainly. If he made trial of the gospel over a period of instruction, tasting and involvement in the church's life, he was assuredly the subject of the Holy Spirit's urgent and repeated pleadings, yet he, after all that, said No, and surely the Spirit was outraged. So out from the church the man goes. He has rejected the one sacrifice that there is for sin. There is nought for him but the 'fury of fire' that is reserved for those who hate God.

Is it 'impossible' to restore the Hollow Man to repentance? Is there no hope that he could even yet come to a real experience of faith? Are those who have made thorough trial of the gospel and then rejected it to be written off entirely? After all, nothing is impossible with God, and that conviction remains at the bottom of our continued prayers for those who turn their backs on Christ. May there not be therefore the exceptional case of the apostate who does find his way back to God? The author may be speaking only of the general rule, and one can see something of how that general rule works. He who trampled the blood of Christ under his feet is psychologically most unlikely to turn to grace even it if continues to be proferred to him. He will think it is impossible that he should be forgiven. Or the rule may work like this: he who has tasted the heavenly gift only to spit it out, may have taken in just enough to be thereafter forever immunised against the good infection of Christ. How hardly therefore shall he enter the kingdom of heaven, if ever.

The Hollow Man solution to the problem of Hebrews 6 and 10, like the Straw Man solution, leaves the doctrine of the perseverance of the saints intact. It is the empty professor of the faith who falls away and suffers the fire of everlasting judgment.

However, we may feel that in order to make the Hollow Man fit the words of Hebrews we have had to exalt him, as it were, far above the ordinary run of folk in our churches today. Were we preachers to find in our people such response as this man made, such drinking in, such receiving with joy, such enlightenment, to say nothing of such participation in the Holy Spirit, would we not feel that something akin to revival had come? Indeed there may now be a fear about our hearts that if such a one as this man is to prove in the end to be a fraud, which of us will stand? This may be no bad fear. We are to take heed, those of us who think we stand, lest we fall (1 Cor. 10:12). But we may also feel that in order to make the words of Hebrews fit our man, we have put them under a strain and forced them out of their natural meaning to make them mean something less than they do.

What, then, of the Man of Tarnished Metal? The metal is silver: pure, solid, hallmarked, genuine. But long neglect has blackened it beyond recognition. Yet silver it remains. So the Man of Tarnished Metal stands for the real Christian, the converted man, the man with the living Christ lodged in his heart. But he has so neglected the gift within him, so turned away from his God and Saviour and so resumed the ways of the world that none would know from their observation of him that he belonged to God at all. Even he himself may believe now that he no longer does. Is it of such a one that Hebrews is speaking?

This time, as we look at the verses we have been studying from Chapters 6 and 10, we find that the description fits easily. There need be no forcing of the words to mean other than what they mean naturally. He was once enlightened, tasted the heavenly gift in the deepest sense, was a partaker of the Holy Spirit, not just in experiencing the manifestations of the Spirit or knowing something of his ordinary operations. He has the Holy Spirit. He has tasted the goodness of the word of God and the powers of the age to come. He has been saved by the power of God, and, without a doubt, he has been sanctified by the blood of the covenant.

Now this man has committed apostasy. He has sinned deliberately. As the New English Bible puts it, he has 'persisted in sin'. It is not just a lapse, nor is it a prolonged bondage to a habit that he hated all the while; it is a determined and deliberate choosing to sin and keeping on at it wilfully. But could a real Christian so behave? G. H. Lang tells the story in his commentary on Hebrews of F. W. Newman, the brother of the man who became the Cardinal. He experienced a conversion to Christ. Some of the most discerning men among the leaders of the Christian Brethren, with whom Newman associated, were fully persuaded that it was genuine. After going on strongly for a time, he about-faced and then for forty years devoted all his considerable talents to doing everything in his power to deflect men and women from Christ. In the miracle grace of God, who can do the impossible, he found repentance at the very end of his life and caused it to be written over his grave that he had died trusting in the precious blood of Christ for salvation. A Christian can sin wilfully after he has received the knowledge of the truth.

What is such a man's fate? F. W. Newman appears to have found repentance, and, if he did, surely he found forgiveness, acceptance with God and in the end everlasting life. But, if we have understood Hebrews correctly, Newman is the exception. The rule is that the apostate will not find repentance but will die in his apostasy. What then is the fate of such a man? Is he lost?

Lang finds a key to understanding this problem in the story of the people of Israel to which the writer of the Epistle refers again and again. In Hebrews 3 allusion is made to the incident in Numbers 13 and 14 when the Israelites, having received the report of the spies about Canaan, refused through unbelief to go up and take the land. Hebrews comments, 'Take care brethren, lest there be in any of you an evil unbelieving heart, leading you to fall away from the living God'

(Hebrews 3:12).

For their falling away the Israelites were thrust back into the wilderness and were never to enjoy the comfort and pleasure of the Promised Land. But they were not thrust back into Egypt, the land that speaks in the Old Testament of separation from God. Indeed, though more than once in their wanderings they longed for Egypt, to that place they were never suffered to return. In the wilderness they remained the objects, almost in spite of themselves, of divine solicitude and overarching care, however much at the same time they suffered under God's grave displeasure and judgment. 'In all their afflictions, he was afflicted, and the angel of his presence saved them.' (Isaiah 63:9).

The application of that to the apostate Christian becomes clear. He is not lost. He cannot be. God has too much respect for the blood of the covenant by which he was sanctified. He is God's child still, and God will not suffer him to be eternally separated from himself. But he will suffer him to live a wilderness life, a wasted life, a life cut off from so many of the blessings he should have enjoyed in Christ. He is not cursed. How can he be? The curse was borne for him once and for all by him Who became a curse for us (Galatians 3:13), but, like the barren field in the author's illustration, he is 'near to being cursed'. This may involve not only a wasted life, but a painful one and perhaps a short one as he suffers hurt and even premature death for his sins.

Scripture is not lacking in illustrations of this in Old Testament and in New. There were the two sons of Aaron in Leviticus 10; Korah and his associates in Numbers 16; Ananias and Sapphira in Acts 5; the hapless persons in Corinth who profaned the Lord's Table and of whom Paul wrote 'That is why many of you are weak and ill, and some have died' (1 Corinthians 11:30); and finally, again in Corinth, the man who was to be 'delivered to Satan for the destruction of his flesh that his soul might be saved in the day of the Lord' (1 Corinthians 5:5). Is that the fate of the apostate Christian, to suffer, perhaps frightfully, in his body, while his soul in the end is saved? The Westminster Confession of Faith speaks of erring Christians so, 'They whom God has accepted in his beloved . . . shall . . . certainly . . . be eternally saved. Nevertheless they may, through the temptation of Satan and of the world, the prevalency of corruption remaining in them, and the neglect of the means of their preservation, fall into grievous sins; and for a time continue therein: whereby they incur God's displeasure, and grieve his Holy Spirit; come to be deprived of some measure of their graces and comforts; and have their hearts hardened, and their consciences wounded; hurt and scandalize others, and bring temporal judgments upon themselves'. (Confession 17:3).

Does the matter end with temporal judgment? G. H. Lang thinks not. For one thing, he considers it would be a patent injustice if such a man as F. W. Newman, who lived comfortably and long and died peacefully in his bed, were, after half a lifetime's deliberate corrupting of the souls of others, to step, by means of an eleventh hour repentance, which could undo little or none of the harm he had perpetrated, straight into the rewards of the blessed like the man who had never veered from the path of faithfulness at all.

Not all will want to echo Lang here. We might lack the courage; or we might lack the conviction, for remembrance of the dying thief in his last-hour conversion, or of the labourers who did receive equal rewards though their stints of service were so varied may make us uneasy with his line of thought.

Lang has a second point that may constrain us to give him more heed. He discovers in his careful and honest examination of the text a difficulty. The man who sinned against the law of Moses was condemned out of the mouths of two witnesses and then sentenced to death by stoning, a hideous way to die. Yet the author says, 'How much worse punishment do you think will be deserved by the man who has spurned the Son of God and profaned the blood of the covenant by which he was sanctified, and outraged the Spirit of grace?' Worse than stoning to death? What could be worse?

This leads him to look into the question of judgment for the unfaithful Christian not only in this life, but in the life to come. Of the final judgment that separates a soul forever from God and casts it into everlasting torment, the Christian can have no experience. He is altogether delivered from that by the atonement Christ made for his sins. But in a passage which is most naturally construed as referring to the people of God, Paul says, 'We must all appear before the judgment seat of Christ, so that each may receive good or evil, according to what he has done.' (2 Corinthians 5:10). Christians generally believe in reward hereafter for their faithfulness on earth. Should they not believe also in loss hereafter for their unfaithfulness on earth? Paul again, speaking this time of the service of the Christian, faithfully done, or neglected, says, 'Now if anyone builds on the foundation with gold, silver, precious stones, wood, hay, stubble — each man's work will become manifest; for the Day will disclose it, because it will be revealed with fire, and the fire will test which sort of work each one has done. If the work which any man has built on the foundation survives, he will receive a reward. If any man's work is burned up, he will suffer loss, though he himself will be saved, but only as by fire.' (1 Corinthians 3:12-15).

Here then, beyond this life, is a fire that will burn away the long-accumulated dross of an apostate's life. The thorns and the thistles of his field are painfully to be purged away, leaving it perhaps happily yet to bear a fairer crop of service in heaven in the end. But whether that be the case or no, for the wretched years of apostasy, he suffers loss, but, through the very Christ whom he denied, but who will not deny him, he will be saved. God will not let him go. He will judge him and it will be a fearful thing for him to fall so into the hands of the living God. But he will be saved.

That then is the Man of Tarnished Metal solution to the problem of apostasy in Hebrews. Better than any other, we may feel, it lets the words of the passages in question mean what they appear to say, and, at the same time accords with the doctrine of the Scriptures as a whole.

May it also be pastorally more satisfactory? We turn back to John Smith. If, in the grace of God, we were to have opportunity to help him back to Christ, which would we prefer to say: 'John, your conversion was not real. You never really received Christ these years ago, but come, receive him now by faith', or 'John, you received Christ as your Saviour these years ago. He has never left you. He is there in your heart now, patiently waiting for the day when you will yield your life to him anew. Let him up from that cellar where you have imprisoned him so long'? I think I would prefer to be able to say the second. The first might carry the risk that John would feel his 'second conversion' was no more authentic than his first is now said to have been. The second honours those early dealings of God with his soul as true and real, and affirms the faithfulness and unspeakable grace of God.

It may be that when we have examined and tested the various solutions, none of them totally satisfies. When in our study of the Scriptures we encounter a persistent difficulty or dissatisfaction, the possibility has to be considered whether we may not be asking the wrong question. We are saying to the author of the Epistle, 'Tell us, what is the eternal fate of the apostate? Assure us that in the end all is well with him. Give us this comfort.' Perhaps the author gives us the answer. But it may be that he yields it to us with difficulty because it is not the thing that he is primarily concerned to say. His concern is not with the apostate. After all, he says it is 'impossible' to do anything with him! His concern is with the man who has not yet fallen but is in terrible danger of doing so. He is not going to say to him, 'Everything will be all right in the end for the apostate, whatever fires may befall him in the interim in time and eternity'. He is urgently, winsomely and with all his heart going to point him to Christ, and to the strength and comfort that are there in the Great High Priest to enable the hard-pressed believer to lift up his drooping hands, strengthen his weak knees, and persevere to the end.

SUFFERING

A Study on Romans 8:18-30

BRIAN MOORE

You live with your head in the sand if you fail to recognize that tragedy, pain, disease, infirmity, sorrow, death are the constant adjuncts of life and never far away from any of us. Nor are Christians immune. Indeed if anything those who pay God scant respect, or dismiss him as irrelevant, whose lives are devious, amoral and evil seem to suffer less. Of course comparisons are notoriously invidious and unreliable for they are usually coloured by our own experience.

Nonetheless this was a question that perplexed the psalmist —

> I envied the arrogant
> > when I saw the prosperity of
> > the wicked.
>
> They have no struggles;
> > their bodies are healthy and
> > strong.
>
> They are free from the
> > burdens common to man;
> > > they are not plagued by
> > human ills.
>
> Therefore pride is their
> > necklace;
> > > they clothe themselves with
> > violence.
>
> From their callous hearts
> > comes iniquity;
> > > the evil conceits of their
> > minds know no limits.
>
> (Psalm 73:3-7)

In other words while it can be argued that unbelievers on the whole *do* suffer less in this life Paul stresses that this should be seen as God's kindness towards them which is intended to lead them to repentance (see Romans 2:4).

Some troubles, however, come upon us (who are Christians) as a specific consequence of our Christian faith. It is this that Jesus alludes to when he warns his disciples, 'In this world you will have trouble' (John 16:33). Not so much in this case pain, disease, infirmity, sorrow or death, but hostility to our Christian stance, the pressure to conform to the standards and behaviour patterns of the world around us, the oppressiveness of evil, the feeling of evil leering at you as you walk past certain establishments, or listen to people talk, or read of a mugging incident, or a dastardly murder, or look at men and women who have

141

become dupes of evil. . . . Or a direct attack of evil, allowed by God, such as Job suffered.

Troubles we all face, then, whichever category they fall into. And nothing provides a sterner test of the reality of our faith. What is to be our response? Some think that the Christian should not turn a hair in trouble. 'There's nothing you can do about it. Just accept it. It is God's will and it is lack of faith that make you question and doubt and waver and hurt. . . .'

Such talk makes one want to cry for it indicates not only a faith that is lacking in sensitivity but a mind that is cocooned from reality. How different is the experience of the psalmists. Here are men (or women) of faith facing up to life and its troubles not with easy equanimity or unquestioning submission but with questions and doubts and a faith that battles through to a trust in God that is real and rugged and enduring.

Take Psalm 55, for example —

Listen to my prayer, O God,
    do not ignore my plea;
    hear me and answer me.
My thoughts trouble me and I
        am distraught
    at the voice of the enemy;
for they bring down suffering
        upon me
    and revile me in their anger.

My heart is in anguish within
    me;
the terrors of death assail
    me.
Fear and trembling have beset
    me.
I said, "Oh, that I had the
        wings of a dove!
    I would flee far away
        and stay in the desert;
I would hurry to my place of shelter,
    far from the tempest and
        storm."

But I call to God,
    and the LORD saves me.
Evening, morning and noon
    I cry out in distress,
    and he hears my voice.
He ransoms me unharmed
    from the battle waged
        against me,
    even though many oppose
        me.

Cast your cares on the LORD
  and he will sustain you;
  he will never let
    the righteous fall.

But as for me, I trust in you.

(Psalm 55:1-8, 16-18, 22, 23).

Or take Jesus in his terrible agony on the cross as (in his human experience) he feels abandoned and cries out Why? Why? (Matt. 27:45, 46). But in his extremity he holds on, not accepting a drink until the job he had been given to do was completed (see John 19:30).

Others think we should praise God for our troubles. But in this regard we can not only be dangerously naive but hideously misled. C. S. Lewis' experience is instructive here. In 1960 after 4 intensely happy years of marriage Lewis' wife, Joy, died of cancer. In an effort to contain his grief and guard himself against losing his faith, he wrote a journal in which he openly expressed his feelings and doubts. A few years later the journal was published under the title, *A Grief Observed*. In the early pages, Lewis writes, 'Not that I am . . . in much danger of ceasing to believe in God. The real danger is coming to believe such dreadful things about him. The conclusion I dread is not "So there's no God after all", but "So this is what God's really like. Deceive yourself no longer".'

It was this conclusion that Job came to at one point in the turmoil of his thoughts after the hammer blows of evil had left him hanging on desperately to the ropes.

How then can I dispute with
  him?
  How then can I find words to
    argue with him?
  Though I were innocent, I
    could not answer him;
I could only plead with my
  Judge for mercy.
Even if I summoned him and
  he responded,
I do not believe he would
  give me a hearing.
He would crush me with a
  storm
and multiply my wounds for
  no reason.
He would not let me regain
  my breath
but would overwhelm me
  with misery

(Job 9: 14-18)

Let me hasten to add that that is not the end of the story, for Job regained his composure and rallied his faith.

What, then, should be our response to suffering, whatever form it takes? In Romans 8:18ff. Paul makes up a number of points which, if grasped, could help us stand fast with the cutting wind of adversity in our face, calm and undeterred, resolute and unafraid.

1 The sufferings of this present life are not worth comparing with the glory that will be revealed in us (v 18).

In Revelation 7 John is given a preview of heaven: 'After this I looked, and behold, a great multitude which no man could number, from every nation, from all tribes and peoples and tongues, standing before the throne and before the Lamb, clothed in white robes, with palm branches in their hands, and crying out with a loud voice, "Salvation belongs to our God . . . and to the Lamb" ' (vv 9-10). 'Who do you think they are?' (v 13). 'You know.' 'They have come out of the troubles of life on earth' (v 14). And in a world where things seem to be growing worse and worse (read 2 Timothy 3:1ff) it's wonderful to look ahead to this future day when 'the troubles . . .' of this life will be left behind. There will be no more hunger, or thirst, no more suffering, or sorrow, or death and we shall live for ever in the glory of Immanuel's land (vv 16-17). This is not mere escapism or pie-in-the-sky-when-you-die romanticism. It is real. There is such a day coming.

This means that whatever dark experiences we pass through in life the sky will lighten and the dawn will break. Disease and death will not have the last word. Pain and suffering will one day be no more, and God will wipe all tears from our eyes.

Even the creation waits in eager anticipation (v 19). For when man rebelled against God's beneficent rule and insisted on living life on his terms as if he were God he brought nature down with him (that is, the sub-human creation) in that it was subjected to 'the frustration of not being able properly to fulfil the purpose of its existence'.

> And, if the question is asked, "What sense can there be in saying that the sub-human creation — the Jungfrau, for example, or the Matterhorn, or the planet Venus — suffers frustration by being prevented from properly fulfilling the purpose of its existence?", the answer must surely be that the whole magnificent theatre of the universe, together with all its splendid properties and all the varied chorus of sub-human life, created for God's glory, is cheated of its true fulfilment so long as man, the chief actor in the drama of God's praise, fails to contribute his rational part. The Jungfrau and the Matterhorn and the planet Venus and all living things too, man alone excepted, do indeed glorify God in their own ways; but since their praise is destined to be not a collection of independent offerings but part of the whole creation, they are prevented from being fully that which they were created to be, so long as man's part is missing, just as all the other players in a concerto would be frustrated of their purpose if the soloist were to fail to play his part.' . . . 'So it is man, not the sub-human creation, which is to blame. . . .
> (C. E. B. Cranfield)

As a result waste, futility and decay in all around we see (v 20). But on the day of revelation or consummation 'the creation itself will be set free from its bondage to decay and obtain the glorious liberty of the children of God' (v 21).

2   The sufferings of this present life are really the birth pangs that precede new life.

Paul now pictures the creation as groaning in travail like a woman in labour (v 22). He thinks, writes a commentator, of 'the suffering of animals — the weak devoured by the strong — the ruthless destruction of plant life, or natural catastrophes of all kinds (e.g. earthquakes, hurricanes, tidal waves, bush fires, volcanoes . . .); he listens to the crying of the wind and sea.' The travail of nature sighing for that moment when it will be, as it were, set free from the crampedness, struggles and frustration of the womb that it knows now, and enter into the freedom, joy and meaningfulness of new life (vv 19, 21).

And we are in the same condition, in travail waiting for the redemption of our bodies (v 23), that is, our full salvation. For although we have renounced our 'we-want-to-run-our-own-lives' spirit and committed ourselves instead to Christ for ever we still live out the new life we have found in him (our 'saved' life) in the context of the old life, that is, in this present body subject to the oppression of evil and the judgment of God and their inevitable concomitant — death which overshadows human life.

This haunting of life by death is vividly illustrated by Tchaikovsky's great B minor Symphony. The music is full of questioning and agitation with the exciting overwhelming rhythms of the march in the penultimate movement giving way to the tragic desolation of the last. James S. Stewart rightly suggests that over against this music of Tchaikovsky should be set, by way of complete contrast, Brahms' Requiem. 'Here death is still the theme, but pessimism there is none, and always the sombre mood merges into the great fortifying climaxes of victory and peace.'

However for the present our final salvation is not yet. Until that day when 'the trumpet will sound . . . and we shall be changed . . . and this perishable nature put on the imperishable, and this mortal nature put on immortality.' (1 Corinthians 15:52-53, cf. also vv 49-50), until that day we groan in travail.

In other words, this world is for the Christian a labour ward where he sighs and groans and suffers until the day of birth the confirmation of his sonship and the redemption of his body, that is, his complete deliverance from 'the principle of sin and death' (see v 2) and its disastrous side effects, and his 'investiture with glory'.

Then the eyes of the blind shall be opened, and the ears of the deaf unstopped; then shall the dumb sing for joy . . . And the ransomed of the Lord shall . . . come to Zion with singing, with everlasting joy upon their heads; they shall obtain joy upon their heads; they shall obtain joy and gladness, and sorrow and sighing shall flee away' (Isaiah 35:5-6, 10).

Nor shall we be disappointed as women in travail sometimes are in that their new-born child is defective, malformed or still-born. For we have the guarantee in our hearts of a full and perfect salvation — the

Holy Spirit (v 23).

Here is the Christian hope, then, face to face with personal suffering and the suffering of our loved ones and our fellowmen and women in this life, that —

> one far off divine event
> to which the whole creation moves

'Then I saw a new heaven and a new earth; for the first heaven and the first earth had passed away, and the sea [the symbol of evil] was no more. And I saw the holy city, new Jerusalem, coming down out of heaven from God, prepared as a bride adorned for her husband; and I heard a great voice from the throne saying, "Behold the dwelling of God is with men. He will dwell with them, and they shall be his people, and God himself will be with them; he will wipe away every tear from their eyes, and death shall be no more, neither shall there be mourning nor crying nor pain any more, for the former things have passed away." And he who sat upon the throne said, "Behold, I make all things new" ' (Revelation 21:1-5 see also 21:22-27, 22:3-5).

We don't see it now. Instead we hope for it and 'wait' for it with patience (vv 24-25). Not stiff upper lip stoical patience but Christian patience, 'patience with the lamp lit' as Tertullian described it in the third century, enduring suffering, despising its shame for the joy that is set before us, like Jesus 'the pioneer and perfector of our faith' (Hebrews 12:2).

3   *The Spirit who is our guarantee of full and perfect salvation is also our Helper, Strengthener, Adviser, and Counsellor (v 26) in the travail of this world.* 'Do not let your hearts be troubled. Trust in God; trust also in me . . . . And I will pray the Father, and he will give you another Counsellor, to be with you for ever . . .' (John 14 1,16). And nowhere is His ministry more significant and potent than in the realm of prayer (vv 26-27).

Previous English translations attribute the sighs or groans of which Paul writes here to the Spirit but John A. T. Robinson suggests that this is not easily intelligible. 'Rather, it is our groanings which the Spirit makes his own. He actually uses our groans as prayers and God the searcher of hearts knows what the Spirit means, because he pleads for God's own people in God's own way . . . . There is an identity between God and the Spirit and an affinity or rapport between the Spirit and our spirits (cf v 16) and this is the secret of Christian prayer. Christian prayer has God on both sides of the relationship! In other words, God by his Spirit, on the one hand, constantly helps us in our weakness and inarticulations in prayer and, on the other, sovereignly works out through our feeble, stammering prayer his good and perfect will.

Whatever the future may hold we have this assurance: 'In everything God works for good with those who love him, who are called according to his purpose', that is, those who have responded to God's saving purpose in Jesus Christ and his call to them in particular by his Spirit, and love him (v 28).

Plainly and starkly this means that many things — even sickness, disease, bereavement, death, disappointment, failure, calamity . . . — God works for our good. Therefore we can sing with John Newton —

> Since all that I meet shall turn to my good,
>   The bitter is sweet, the medicine is food!
> Though painful at present, 'twill cease before long,
>   And then, O how pleasant the conqueror's song!

That is to say we recognize that suffering has its use in God's scheme of things. For example:

(1) Suffering keeps us humble. The shattering blows that hammered Job in rapid succession left him a humbled man.

> Naked I came from my mother's womb
>   and naked I shall depart.
> The LORD gave and the LORD
>   has taken away;
> may the name of the LORD
>   be praised.

And Malcolm Muggeridge has written: 'Supposing you eliminated suffering, what a dreadful place the world would be! . . . because everything that corrects the tendency of . . . man to feel over-important and over-pleased with himself would disappear. He's bad enough now, but he would be absolutely intolerable if he never suffered'.

(2) Suffering disciplines us. Whatever we experience in the realm of suffering should be thought of as part of 'the present discipline whereby God teaches us patience, courage, humility, faithfulness, and similar lessons' (J. I. Packer).

> My son, do not make light of
>   the Lord's discipline,
> and do not lose heart when
>   he rebukes you,
> because the Lord disciplines
>   those whom he loves,
> and he punishes everyone he
>   accepts as a son.
>
> (Hebrews 12:5, 6)

'He cuts off every branch in me that bears no fruit, while every branch that does bear fruit he trims clean so that it will be even more fruitful'. John 15:2

'Before I was afflicted I went astray, but now I obey your word'. 'It was good for me to be afflicted so that I might learn your decrees'. Psalm 119:67, 71

(3) Suffering produces character and refines faith. 'Not only so, but we also rejoice in our suffering, because we know that suffering produces perseverance; perseverance, character; and character, hope' (James 1:2, 3).

'In this you greatly rejoice, though now for a little while you may have had to suffer grief in all kinds of trials. These have come so that your faith — of greater worth than gold, which perishes even though refined by fire — may be proved genuine and may result in praise, glory and honour when Jesus Christ is revealed' (Peter 1:6, 7).

4   *God's purpose in our salvation is not our health, or comfort, or happiness but our like-ness to Christ (v 29).* And that purpose, as Paul makes explicit, has its roots in God's choice in eternity, which is the meaning of predestination.

Clearly this teaching is beyond our minds to understand. But one thing we can affirm. All too often predestination is discussed and argued about as an abstract theological dogma which makes nonsense of man's moral responsibility. That is the wrong atmosphere in which to try to get to grips with it. For it is pre-eminently a doctrine of experience, something we come to learn as we commit ourselves to our Creator God and Lord and his Son our Saviour.

> I sought the Lord, and afterward I knew
>   He moved my soul to seek Him, seeking me;
> It was not I that found, O Saviour true —
>   No, I was found by Thee.
>
> Thou didst reach forth Thy hand and mine enfold;
>   I walked and sank not on the storm-vexed sea —
> 'Twas not so much that I on Thee took hold,
>   As Thou, dear Lord, on me.
>
> I find, I walk, I love, but O the whole
>   Of love is but my answer, Lord, to Thee;
> For Thou wast long beforehand with my soul,
>   Alway Thou lovedst me.

In essence that is what predestination means. Notice that in detailing the steps between God's choice of us in eternity and our final redemption Paul jumps from our calling by God at a specific point in time and his acquittal of us for Christ's sake (our justification) which marked the beginning of our Christian life to our glorification leaving out the whole of our Christian experience (v 30). As if to say, 'Your trials, adversities and sufferings in the maelstrom of life may be baffling and sore and grievous but glory is just around the corner. Of that you can be absolutely, incontrovertibly sure.'

A. M. Toplady put it into memorable words —

> My name from the palms of His hands
>   Eternity will not erase;
> Impressed on His heart it remains,
>   In marks of indelible grace.
> Yes, I to the end shall endure,
>   As sure as the earnest [the guarantee,
>   the Holy Spirit] is given;
> More happy, but not more secure,
>   The glorified spirits in heaven.

148